# Changing Communities

# Changing Communities

## Church from the grassroots

JEANNE HINTON AND PETER B. PRICE

CHURCHES TOGETHER
IN BRITAIN AND IRELAND

Churches Together in Britain and Ireland
Inter-Church House
35-41 Lower Marsh
London SE1 7SA
Tel. +44 (0) 20 7523 2121; Fax +44 (0) 20 7928 0010
info@ctbi.org.uk or (team)@ctbi.org.uk
www.ctbi.org.uk

ISBN 0 85169 284 2

Published 2003 by Churches Together in Britain and Ireland

Produced by Church House Publishing

Further copies available from CTBI Publications, 31 Great Smith Street,
London SW1P 3BN; Tel: +44 (0) 20 7898 1300; Fax: +44 (0) 20 7898 1305;
orders@ctbi.org.uk   www.chbookshop.co.uk

Cover designed by Church House Publishing

Printed by Creative Print and Design Group, Ebbw Vale, Wales

# Contents

# Foreword

## Churches as small-scale conspiracies of hope

As in every age, the most creative exponents of the Christian message have often been those who think small. In faith they immerse themselves in everyday life, they work humbly to build a church that lives up to the message of the gospel that created it, and they exemplify its transforming impact on the wider community in a thousand unseen ways. That is the process of incarnation, of Word becoming flesh. It is a costly path that will always be central for followers of Jesus Christ, those who experience the new reality declared in his decisive relationship to God and in the world-changing events of his life, death and resurrection.

In the middle of a culture that instead emphasizes technocratic problem-solving, material success and fleeting image, such a modest way of 'being church' is often hidden, submerged or sidelined. It does not generate appropriate 'news values' for television. It frequently gets buried in the plans, procedures and politics of institutional life, not least those of our church structures. It is demanding and difficult to sustain. It makes uneven ripples where we might prefer dramatic, headline-generating waves.

For these and many other reasons it has been common to ignore or overlook the true significance of stories, experiences and methods emerging from small Christian communities. Why bother with paltry mustard seeds (Matthew 13.31-32) in an age of transnational agribusiness? What hope do small communities offer when faced with the mass decline of inherited church institutions in our increasingly diverse, de-Christianized, consumerist and spiritually eclectic societies?

From the viewpoint of the gospel to think like this is a profound mistake. The domination-free kingdom of God is necessarily revealed at the margins of our expectations. The size of the challenge facing the churches today should certainly never be underestimated. But to attempt a re-engineering of existing denominational and ecumenical structures 'from above' *without* the life, energy and (above all) people-based connectedness flowing from below is to fall prey to the illusion of managerialism. This is not only out of step with the values of Jesus Christ, it is also increasingly out of touch with the 'network society' emerging in today's media-driven, post-modern world.

## Participants in change

Peter Price and Jeanne Hinton have for many years been active participants in what they write about here. Their lives have taken different directions. Peter ended up heading a major Anglican missionary society, USPG. He became area Bishop of Kingston and he is now the diocesan Bishop of Bath and Wells in the Church of England. Jeanne has continued her ecumenical work of writing, workshop leading and actively supporting local Christian communities, in Britain and Ireland and in other parts of Europe and the world too.

For Peter also the experience of grassroots church and theology in Latin America, Africa and Asia has been foundational in re-thinking what it means to 'be church'. Both have lived and breathed the air of practical ecumenism, of the link between evangelical commitment and Christian catholicity. I have been privileged to work with both of them over the years. Some time ago the three of us called a group of friends together at the London Mennonite Centre to discern where our journeys might coincide in the future. At the time it was none too clear. But the fruits of Christian community rarely are at first sight. We have to look again.

Jeanne and Peter have done just that by continually revisiting and developing the resources for small-scale hope in the Christian story. In recent times their paths have been bound together with that of New Way, a group of friends and collaborators who have been as much concerned with the 'how to' of Christian community as with the 'what and where'. That is why this book has a distinctly hands-on feel. While no one is suggesting that solutions in one local context can simply be transferred to another, or that someone else can 'do it for you', it is inescapably the case that we must learn from one another in the global-and-local community that is the Church.

This is often profoundly difficult in practice. There is something about contemporary culture that looks for quick solutions or migrates too rapidly from one 'experience' to another. Commitment, self-help, partnership and a lay-centred involvement are difficult to maintain. What this book and the practical wisdom behind it suggests is that they are, however, essential.

If this is so our ways of doing things cannot remain static or located in a romantic past. Tradition is there to move us forward, not to hold us back. That is one danger in books of stories. They can leave us with a warm glow about the historic movement of the Spirit in the smallness of human scale. But they do not necessarily spur us to action or response today. However, by bridging the gap between narrative and know-how, Jeanne and Peter encourage all of us to take short, realizable steps of faith, rather than only to admire from afar.

## Future church

Where, then, do we go from here? The answer lies in the hands of the reader. It is up to you and me. Though there are many friends along the way, there is no 'someone else' who will magically sort it out for us. But the contours of our future hope – of Future Church – can be seen in outline in many places, in crossroads that only become apparent as we navigate them.

First, I would mention the fascinating but often unexplored links between the kind of ecumenical small Christian community initiatives described here and the vitality of 'new' or 'house' churches from the evangelical and charismatic movements. In the past they have been deeply divided by theology and culture. Some of that has changed, but there are persistent differences still. Christians are agreed that Jesus Christ makes 'all the difference in the world', but we have continued (and will continue) to argue about the nature, scope and implications of that difference. Some have retreated into exclusivity, for example. Others have embraced an unfocused openness that lacks a cutting edge.

In the face of intra-Christian difficulties there has nevertheless been increasing positive traffic in all directions between the ecumenical, evangelical, Catholic and pentecostal-charismatic streams of Christianity. This is God's way of keeping us open; of stopping us from mistaking our limited perceptions for God's eternal purposes. The lives of Peter and Jeanne exemplify that. They show us that in many local situations Christians of different temperaments and theologies have learned to respect rather than suspect one another. Those involved in community-based church initiatives have often recognized a certain convergence in ground-up methodology, for instance, and in the acknowledgement that 'emergent' forms of church pose a necessary challenge to those 'inherited' forms that have relied too heavily on cultural accretion and upon the idea of a church *for* rather than *of* the people. The liberating claims of Christ have made themselves known in fresh and unexpected ways.

Second, there are distinct overlaps between the stories and methods described here, in the work of New Way of Being Church, and in the experience of the missionary congregation and community-building approach of 'Building Bridges of Hope' (BBH), an initiative of the CTBI Churches' Commission on Mission. BBH is described along with other resources at the end of this book and in Jeanne Hinton's previous book for CTBI, *Changing Churches* (2002). It has proceeded along two important lines. One is *action-research*, which closely ties together analysis and practical support, so that it can become a 'living laboratory' for changing churches. The other is *accompaniment*, the simple but demanding process of guiding each other over a significant period of time. The evidence of BBH, New Way and other similar experiments is that mentors and associates are the way forward, not prescriptions and blueprints.

Third, at the heart of what you read here is deep spirituality: people whose lives have changed, who have embraced the changes around them Christianly, and who can therefore assist others in the changing process. But in order to ride the waves of innovation or to make the most of what we have inherited through first-line churches, we have to be connected and nourished. It is security that enables risk. This is what prayer is all about. It centres us, then draws us out of ourselves and in the direction of our neighbours. It creates an orientation towards the Christ-like God who beckons us with the promise of new life, personally and socially. Equally, worship is a distinctive discipline that shapes a community towards divine hope, distinguishing for us what is really worth-it-full (worshipful), what is truly valuable. It enables us both to affirm and to resist, as necessary. It creates small-scale, mustard seed conspiracies of hope.

Sometimes, though, faithful Christians despair of the Church. It can drain our energy and fuel our rage in its awkwardness and imperfection. The trouble is we cannot do without it. The gospel is a communal, incarnational hope. It has been handed down in community. It requires companionship. And it concerns the remaking of persons-in-relationship, not the spiritualized extraction of individuals from the midst of everyday life. This book will renew our belief that the Church is genuinely *possible* in those quite ordinary ways out of which an extraordinary grace is born. As the Mennonite theologian John Driver has said, it is an 'experimental plot' for God in human history. Or as the Catholic writer Edith Barnard has proposed, the Church is called to exist as 'a model house for the kingdom of God'. In the stories and practicalities which Jeanne and Peter offer us here we see how this can be not a tyrannical ideal but a viable option.

Simon Barrow
Secretary
Churches' Commission on Mission
Churches Together in Britain and Ireland

# Acknowledgements

The authors would like to thank a number of people: In particular, Tony Barker, Frances Hawkey, Anne Hope, Pauline Lamming, Dee Price, Magdalen Smith, Carol Stickland and John Summers, for allowing their stories told in *A Tapestry of Stories* and other New Way booklets to be edited and included here and thus to weave a background tapestry for this book.

There are many others whose stories are mentioned or alluded to, or whose wisdom is shared. In this we acknowledge the contribution of so many to changing communities, and not least members of the New Way team, who are integral to the story told in these pages. We are grateful to the Churches' Commission on Mission (CCOM) of Churches Together in Britain and Ireland for bringing this work, and its predecessor, *Changing Churches* (CTBI, 2002) to publication.

CTBI/CCOM and the authors also very much appreciate the speed and efficiency with which Church House Publishing (and especially Sarah Roberts, Linda Foster, Andy Stonehouse and Kate Hughes) have enabled this book to be produced.

There is one other person to be mentioned – Simon Barrow. It is due to his encouragement and support that the four New Way booklets that make up this book are now available for a wider readership. It is one result too of a collaborative friendship over many years, which Simon writes about in his Foreword. It is, we believe, out of these networks of friendship and shared vision that change most often comes, from these beginnings more than any other. Simon's way of offering friendship and encouragement to many is an invaluable gift; we thank him for it.

# Introduction

In a small Devon village parishioners gather around a map as part of their weekly meeting as a church. They are 'mapping' their community, discovering together the boundaries of their parish, where people live, the school, farms, shops, village hall and other places where people gather. At the same time they tell stories, share news, highlight issues and problems that face the community or individuals. They are re-learning what it is to be 'church' – not only as a gathered congregation, but as those who are seeking the well-being of their community in the name of Jesus Christ.

This is a book about the place of small Christian communities in today's world. It tells some stories and provides some practical ideas for creating, developing and maintaining communities of faith and witness in our time. The Church today is undergoing change. Although fewer people overall attend church services, the quality of Christian commitment has probably never been higher amongst those who do.

Today's world presents the Christian community with many challenges and opportunities. In Britain people by and large no longer know the basics of the Christian faith, such as the festivals of the Church and their meaning, nor the story of Jesus, or the accounts of people of God in the Bible. Similarly, people do not know the commandments of Jesus: 'love your neighbour as yourself', 'love your enemies', 'forgive . . . as you are forgiven'.

All of this presents both a challenge and an opportunity for the Christian Church of all denominations. How do we bear witness to neighbours, school friends, colleagues? Ours has been an age in which individualism, people's rights and personal choice have been the priorities for many. This has been mirrored in our church life and patterns of Christian living. The emphasis on personal faith, and in some churches the receiving of spiritual gifts, are both valuable in themselves but have nevertheless led to an inwardness, an exclusivity. Yet at the same time many seek to share their faith and to win neighbours and friends to follow Christ.

In other parts of the Church and the world, the emphasis on personal faith has been tempered by a growing concern for establishing models of Christian living that reflect God's justice and the making of peace, seeking to provide communities of reconciliation in places of pain and dislocation. Such communities offer a sense of belonging and an atmosphere for the healing of hurts, care for the needy and the possibility of hope.

Whatever our starting point on the Christian journey, the task of the people of God is to 'make Christ known'. The core of Jesus' teaching was the bringing of God's rule or kingdom into human affairs. This rule or way of living was to be marked by loving, just and peaceful human relationships with other human beings, the creation and God. In the Holy Trinity, this relationship is modelled between Father, Son and Holy Spirit – Creator, Redeemer and Life-giver.

Today we live in a world where there are few absolutes, where the certainties about right and wrong, good and bad, have given way to relativity, where there is a danger of thinking or saying, 'It is only wrong if I think it is wrong.' Of course, this is an oversimplification, but it exposes something of the danger of our individualistic 'me' culture. What is missing in so many places is a sense of belonging, of community; and with that absence of community goes an absence of responsibility, care, or love for 'neighbour'.

The Church remains in a unique position to provide an antidote to individualism, to lack of community. However individualistic people's faith may become, few Christians would deny the need to meet with others for worship and fellowship. Admittedly, all too often that can take on a 'club-like' atmosphere and newcomers can find it difficult to gain entry, particularly if they do not have any experience of church culture. Yet the basis of community is there, and elements of the gospel are practised in daily living.

The early Church was frequently born in a rural environment, but famine, war, debt, persecution and other difficulties often forced people into the labour-hungry cities of the Roman Empire. It was here that the churches to which Paul, Peter, James and others wrote their letters began to flourish and grow. Many Christians were poor, often they were slaves or little more than hired hands. The First Letter of Peter is written to such people and he calls them 'foreigners, or sojourners, without citizenship'. These folk had no rights, no protection from the law, and were frequently treated as little more than goods and possessions. Their faith in Jesus Christ not only sustained them, but also empowered them to be amongst the most courageous witnesses to the power of God at work in the world.

For many, their gospel practices were simple courtesies. They demonstrated the power of God through their love for one another and their attention to the practice of forgiveness, confessing their sins, seeking to live their faith by kind actions, sincerity and neighbourliness, and being careful not to become anxious about tomorrow's problems. For some people this may not seem very revolutionary, but when we look at the things that divide human society, the diligent practice of such virtues becomes quite impressive, and where words cannot be spoken, actions speak.

As these groups of people organized themselves into churches, they sought to look after not only their own, but also, and particularly, those in similar circumstances. Citizenship in the Roman Empire was granted and could be bought. The indigenous citizens without rights who were the first Christians saw themselves as 'citizens of the kingdom of God' – and as such they sought the welfare of the people around them, partly by sharing their meagre resources, but above all by the practice of simple loving acts.

Jesus' strategy for mission was based on the offer of hope to the sick and those oppressed by 'demons', discrimination, or other forms of exclusion. Whatever modern interpretation we give to his concerns, what they represent for today's Church is still the core of its mission. Jesus built communities of faith, beginning with his discipleship group; through the activity of the Spirit at Pentecost, the Church then developed out of such small communities. We believe that small communities which are committed to the mission strategy of Jesus and which seek to re-build, re-make and re-interpret community are a significant way forward for the Church today.

The material in this book has been drawn largely from four small booklets published by New Way in 1998/9, two written by Peter and two by Jeanne. One of Jeanne's was an edited book of stories, *A Tapestry of Stories*, and excerpts from this book are included in this one as illustrative material. There are a number of stories told in this book, weaving together material from many different sources. We are grateful to all those who have contributed to this book in this way.

Over the past 30 or 40 years we have tried to discover models of church which recognize the place of all, even the youngest, both as learners and teachers, and to discover and nurture churches as communities of learning, places where conflicts are resolved and peacemaking and care for the environment are tackled on a day-to-day basis at a local level. In New Way we frequently discuss whether this is something that should be done within the institutional churches, or outside of them. It is an ongoing debate, which we find creative. Those of us who regard the small Christian community as a model of the Church at the local level can see its worth to the parish or local church structure as a means of mission as well as nurture and support. Others see small Christian communities as places where people who have become disillusioned with the institutional church can find support, encouragement and a focus for work in the community.

As a bishop, Peter perhaps inevitably represents the view that small Christian communities can be the means of nurturing and strengthening the mission of the local parish church. While embracing that position, Jeanne also strongly affirms the contribution of those groups which exist more on the margins of the institutional church, as a kind of 'prophetic edge'. The debate continues! In writing this book, we have tried to be objective, but the discerning reader will notice from time to time which influence is dominating the discussion.

However, we are both convinced that God can use anyone and anything, and we find considerable consolation in the words of an Iona hymn:

> Build from the human fabric, signs
> Of how your kingdom thrives,
> Of how the Holy Spirit changes life,
> By changing lives.[1]

We trust that the reflections that follow will bring about changed lives and communities, for the sake of Jesus Christ.

# 1

# Flowers along the path

It was Sunday and there was a Fun Run for charity in the village. A member of the New Way team was on her way to church, late. Now she was held up. Crowds lined the road waiting for the runners to pass. All the village organizations were there with their stalls; the Fun Run was drawing people together, creating a sense of community. 'But where are the Christians?' thought Pauline in dismay. 'In church with their backs to it all!' She decided then and there to stay and support the run.

This story usually draws a wry smile from those who hear it. It touches on a truth we don't like to hear. Too often the Church is not involved in the everyday concerns of people, not felt to be part of the community. This book is about getting involved in our local communities, about responsible citizenship in today's world, about making a difference, about living the good news.

Many are already doing it.

A small congregation had to abandon its building for lack of funds. The expectation was that they would link up with another congregation, but the people chose instead to break the mould and take the opportunity and time to re-evaluate what it meant for them to be church in the local community. They started to meet in a small community centre based on a former council flat. After a time this too was closed and the invitation came to meet in the local pub – outside opening hours!

One member writes: 'As a small Christian community we have grown individually and collectively in our faith and commitment in a way that I have not experienced before in a larger or more conventional church . . . together we wrestle with the gospel in the reality of our lives, and with our lives in the reality of the gospel.'[1]

Some members of a Roman Catholic religious order decided to relocate their community to an Urban Priority Area in South London. Two members brought invaluable experience from time spent as missionary sisters in South America, where they had worked in one of the poorer districts of a large city. In South London they were joined by people from other Christian traditions and together they set about encouraging the formation of a small Christian community in one of the blocks on the estate. At first they met to share their common experience of coping daily with vandalism and violence and the feeling of having been abandoned by the authorities.

> Each time the group met, people shared something of their own life from the previous week. In addition everyone was encouraged to recount their own history.

> The group tried to find things to celebrate when it met – a birthday, success at getting a job, the return of someone from holiday. The problems of the neighbourhood were always a concern, and some attempt was made to identify an area of concern, and plan some action that would contribute to changing things a little.[2]

In an inner-city area of Birmingham in the late 1980s a number of people from various Christian congregations found themselves independently exercised about what was happening in their neighbourhood. Money was being poured into the area for regeneration, but for whose benefit? Local inhabitants feared it was not for theirs. Those concerned about the situation anticipated that it would be the most disadvantaged who would in the end bear the cost of the area's regeneration programme.

Some of these people worked for local agencies, most of them lived or worked in the area. They came together rather haphazardly through conversations on street corners and over the telephone. Particular questions kept surfacing. One was 'How can we be, and build, a people of hope?' Gradually other people came and joined the original nine, and another small Christian community was born.

We feel that God is not so much leading as confronting us, deep within our being . . . We feel that the reign of God is not a horizon, but a wellspring of life in the nitty-gritty day-to-day loose ends of life.[3]

As these stories show, small Christian communities can start in many different ways. Others have started through a group of people meeting at a workshop on homelessness, or as a result of a Lenten Bible study group, or through an advertisement put in a newspaper. Usually small communities begin because of the initiative of one person or just a few people, who may be laypeople or ministers, priests or religious sisters or brothers, who believe that small communities are integral to their understanding of church.

Some communities begin through people sharing a common concern to do with an issue such as fair trade, poverty, unemployment or a more simple lifestyle. Most often, however, two or three people come together with a desire to share in prayer and concern for others. This is at the heart of what church is about. Whatever the starting point, each community begins and develops differently, unique and distinct from every other. This book emphasizes the small Christian community – how to start, how to go on, how to be effective. We recognize that for some people finding or starting such a community is not always easy or even possible. There may be too few people interested, or a start is made and people move away at a critical moment and the group becomes untenable. Sometimes the local church itself may discourage such a move or perhaps it just isn't the right time to establish a group. But as the longest journey begins with one step, so there are steps, often small, that anyone can take to begin making a difference in their neighbourhood, community or church. We hope this book will offer some helpful examples.

# A kind of longing

Begin with the dream. What do you want to see happen? What changes? With whom?

When Peter completed his theological training 25 years ago, he was looking for a parish to begin ministry. He had been offered a job working in the local school as chaplain for half a week, as well as trying to build a new congregation on the neighbouring housing estate, which was shortly to be enlarged by overspill development from the city of Portsmouth; but he turned the post down. During a short holiday he had a dream. He dreamt about the housing estate and how, in each of the streets, there was a small group of people trying to live out a Christian way of life. He woke convinced that he should see whether the Vicar, whose offer he had turned down, would reconsider him. The Vicar did, and within four years there was not only a thriving congregation meeting in the local school, but also – just as in the dream – small neighbourhood groups meeting together.

Much later in their lives and ministry in a difficult parish situation, Peter's wife Dee had a different kind of dream. She tells it in this way:

> I was visiting a religious community of men, women and children in the country. With me were several people from the cathedral. Those who were with me were not all pleased to be there. Most of them expected to be going to the pub – but the person in the dream who met us took us to the religious community. In the community there was a woman who did tricks! One of her tricks was to lie under a rug on the floor and to appear so flat that she could make people believe there was no one there at all! She could also shape the rug so that it looked like a house, a car or a cat!
>
> Another old lady said she was terrified when she first came to the community, but she became the most wonderful and appreciated teacher. The man in charge of the community was constantly having to go to his home because it kept getting flooded. I asked whether the community was solvent. 'It was until people from the cathedral came,' he said. 'But no one from the cathedral has paid.'
>
> Leaving the community I went towards the nearby church, but it was closed because the way to it was too dangerous.

The path leading to it was cluttered with broken beds, bicycles and chairs. When people met to worship they were addressed by a man who threw his riding boots into the congregation! No one knew who was going to get hit! As I turned to leave, I noticed that all the paths to the houses lived in by the community had beautiful grass and flowers.

A dream analyst would no doubt have fun with those two dreams! But they throw some light on the challenges that confront us in making a difference in today's world. 'I have a dream', declared Martin Luther King, and out of it the Civil Rights movement in the USA was born. In the 1970s and 1980s throughout Latin America many priests and religious 'dreamed' of a theology of life and models of church that would make God's love real and enable people to live lives of hope and dignity. A priest who works in Brazil's *favelas* describes how one day in the city he observed a flower blooming through a crack in the concrete roadway. For him this was a parable of small communities as 'a new way of being church'. Or, as in Dee's dream, flowers along the path.

In Britain, Europe and the USA during those two decades there were many alternative lifestyle communities. Some, like Sojourners in Washington DC, Celebration in Houston, Post Green in Dorset and reconciliation communities such as Corrymeela in Northern Ireland and Iona in Scotland, continue to this day. In addition there were many experiments in so-called lifestyle communities, and although most of them were short-lived, a kind of longing, a dreaming, was awakened from them.

During the 1980s and 1990s many priests and religious, particularly in Ireland, returned after years of working in missionary situations with alternative structures such as the base ecclesial communities. These models of church – grassroots church communities – focused strongly on the poor and influenced the creation of theologies of liberation. In their homeland, these returning missionaries discovered a church on the wane, self-evidently failing to bring love, hope and justice to the most vulnerable and marginalized. Many of them settled in

5

housing estates and inner-city neighbourhoods and began applying the principles they had learned 'in the missions' to their own people.

For the past 30 or 40 years we have been among those who have 'dreamed' and worked for a church *of* the people rather than *for* the people. Jeanne's experience began in the late 1950s through her work with young people in youth clubs in South London. During the 1950s and 1960s she came together with other Christian youth leaders across Britain to found the Frontier Youth Trust, an organization that continues to work with young people on the edges of society. The 'church in the club' was born in those early years – a place where young people who found faith could grow and develop, bridging the gap between them and a church where, even at its best, they didn't feel at home. To Jeanne, 'club church' had and has much in common with the basic ecclesial communities she has come to know in more recent years.

Peter has also worked with others at different times and places, creating small church communities. Sometimes these have been ecumenical activities on inner-city estates, where people have few expectations of the Church, and denominationalism is of little consequence. He has seen people like the old lady in Dee's dream arrive frightened but emerge as wonderfully creative facilitators, nurturers, even teachers. Peter's experience on the estate where his ministry began remains with him, particularly the sense that the path to the Church is 'cluttered', if not with 'broken beds, old bicycles and chairs', then with an obsession about itself and an inertia over change that leaves the *status quo* intact and keeps religion privatized and pietistic. Many people are tired of a church leadership that seems to 'throw riding boots into the congregation' and have had enough of 'being hit'. For many the Church is 'too dangerous'. We have lost a sense of conviction religion – the conviction of the first Christians – that sees church as a community of free citizens who seek the welfare of the neighbourhood. This original meaning of the word 'church' will be considered in greater depth in the next chapter.

# 2

# What is church?

When Peter began his ministry on the housing estate in Portsmouth there was no church building and no congregation – no church, in fact. For a number of years a piece of land had been earmarked for a church building and marked with a wooden sign. When Peter and Dee arrived, the sign had gone and its demise had become part of the folk-lore of the local community. After some months of energetic visiting, offering hospitality to people by inviting them to meet their neighbours over a simple supper, a service of worship was established in one of the local schools. Many people came and it was a time of considerable excitement.[1]

At the same time a new housing development was springing up on land adjoining the original church site. Enthusiastically, members of the fledgling congregation set out to make their new neighbours welcome. This took some courage, as the prevailing wisdom was that this overspill estate would be filled with people who would be 'nothing but trouble'. Bunches of flowers, biscuits and cakes were offered to people 'as soon as the curtains went up in the windows' and a leaflet was also given to the newcomers, welcoming them and telling them where to find doctors, schools, shops and buses.

After a few weeks it became apparent that none of the people visited came to Sunday worship in the local school. Some of the congregation felt disappointed; others, more phlegmatically, observed that 'we weren't out to get them to church'. Still others wondered if there was a reason why people didn't come. One afternoon, as Peter was wandering the streets, a woman from one of the new houses invited him in. 'You probably think we are terrible not coming to church,' she began. 'Most of us have never been made to feel more welcome in a place. But you see,' she said, 'the reason we don't come to church is that we wouldn't know what to do if we came.'

Intuitively, this woman and her neighbours understood that churches, however new and welcoming, have a culture that informs their way of life. She and her friends wanted to belong, they liked what they had seen and experienced of the local church, but they did not believe that they had access to its lifestyle and values. As a result of this encounter, the woman agreed to gather a few of her neighbours together to meet with Peter and some of the congregation in order to explore the matter further.[2] This woman's action was in itself counter-cultural; many of the newcomers had been rehoused from estates where your burglar was most likely your neighbour! Later, a pattern of small neighbourhood groups was developed to help people make the long journey from welcome into the community to participation in the life of the church.

Peter's reflection on this experience is that the newness of the situation enabled these steps to be taken. In a more traditional parish this could probably not have taken place without a radical restructuring of the church's life. This raises some questions: What is church? And what (and who) is church for?

## What is church?

Nowadays the term 'church' is usually associated with a religious gathering, although sometimes political parties and other groups describe themselves as 'a broad church'. In the Greek and Roman Empires, however, 'church' was a secular term. It meant simply a gathering, a meeting or, more precisely, a gathering of those called out or elected. In the Roman Empire 'ecclesia' or 'church' was a political term particularly associated with community organization, a gathering of free citizens who worked for the welfare of the neighbourhood. These citizens were responsible for seeing that the will of the authorities was put into practice in all matters concerning law and order, social behaviour and allegiance to the Emperor.

Through its gatherings, its 'ecclesia', the fledgling Christian community also looked after the welfare of its people (Acts 4.34; 6.1-6), although their allegiance was to Jesus Christ rather than the Emperor. This community gave its witness in the day-to-day practice of 'little virtues': refusing to draw attention to oneself (Luke 14.7-10; Mark 10.45; Romans 12.10), being sincere (Matthew 5.37), being discreet and knowing when to speak and when to keep silence (James 3.3-10; Matthew 18.15), avoiding anxiety and preoccupation with the future (Matthew 6.32-34), being pleasant (Matthew 6.16) and always wanting to do good (Romans 12.51), being on time (Matthew 25.1-13), avoiding laziness and inactivity (Matthew 20.1-16), persevering and sticking with the faith through thick and thin (Luke 9.62; Matthew 24.13; 25.21).

These familiar and everyday things were important in the household community churches. Living out these demanding 'little virtues' of hearth and home were essential in a society where little value was placed on such things,[3] and where mobility was relatively limited. People had a small sphere of influence; they normally only travelled short distances except in extreme situations such as war, persecution, famine or economic necessity.

## What is 'church' for?

The secular model of a church was not the only model of gathering and seeking the welfare of the neighbourhood known to the early Christians. Many Christians of the first congregations emerged from the synagogue model of community. Limited to Jews and proselytes of the Jewish faith, the formation of a synagogue (gathering) required the agreement of ten rabbis or teachers of the Law. However, those who met in the name of Jesus as a church (gathering) could be formed 'whenever (any!) two or three are gathered together' (Matthew 18.20).

Despite risks to their integrity, the danger of betrayal and the ever-present possibility of heresy and apostasy, early Christian communities were inclusive and accepting of all. This was a source of attraction in itself (Acts 2.42-47; 4.32-34). The evident power of God present amongst the believers caused some to want membership in order to inherit their portion of that power (Acts 8.9-24), and of course there were those who sought benefits without responsibility (Acts 5.1-11).

Many of the earliest Christians were refugees. Matthew's gospel was written for the Christian Diaspora who fled from various persecutions to the city of Antioch – where followers of the (Jesus) Way were first called Christians. The First Letter of Peter was written to 'the exiles of the Dispersion' (1 Peter 1.1) in Pontus, Galatia, Cappadocia, Bithynia and elsewhere. The growth of cities and the decline of rural economies meant that huge numbers of people were on the move. Some of these were groups of Christians who felt depressed, discouraged and isolated. The letters of Peter and other New Testament writings were written for the encouragement of those in exile (1 Peter 1.17).

People in an alien culture and environment need practical encouragement in terms of down-to-earth advice. Their lives are to be a good example (witness) to those who do not know God, and practice (rather than preaching) is what really sustains and makes faith come alive (1 Peter 3.2). Daily humiliations were to be borne humbly, patiently and obediently by those who were little more than household slaves, subject to their 'masters' (1 Peter 2.18). No other options existed for them, either economically or spiritually. When gathered in their own communities as 'God's household', however, they were challenged to demonstrate this new order through mutual self-giving expressed lovingly and generously in the 'charisms' of serving others (1 Peter 4.10).[4]

# Weaving the tapestry

Zion Baptist Church was, and still is, a tiny church.[5] True, it has huge buildings built in 1837 and 1879, but the number of people is very small. In the early 1990s there had been discussion about closing the church building and congregations dispersing. Then the young minister left. Set in the centre of the city, once surrounded by hundreds of family houses, long demolished, the church faced a desperate situation. Many of the members of the church had left for the larger and more flourishing churches in the city. A fragile, weak and fearful group were left, with little hope but to hang on and stay.

Elsewhere and independently, God was prompting six people to consider moving to Zion, with a specific vision for the local community . . . First the call of God came to six, then to other individuals, usually without any human prompting. Over five years, hundreds of visitors have come to visit the church and its projects, sometimes just to look and see what the Lord is doing. Others have stayed, wanting to participate in a tiny community that has dedicated itself to the poor and often marginalized where the living presence of Christ has been discovered in a new way.

One gospel project leads to another. Cambridgeshire Social Services and the City Council asked the church to begin a community transport scheme 'because we have seen how your church cares for people'. Research had discovered that there were about 7,000 people in the city who could not use public transport due to physical disability. Cambridge Dial-a-Ride has now been operating for two years, has purchased four buses with plans for two more, providing 13,600 journeys . . . The small Zion church community has come to understand church as seven days a week, twenty-four hours a day.

Tony Barker, *A Tapestry of Stories*

# Who is 'church' for?

We have already indicated that the earliest Christian communities, unlike their Jewish counterparts, sought to include any who wanted to join them, whatever the risks. Was the distribution of provisions to the widows, for example, which became such a major task for the early Jerusalem Church (Acts 6.1-5), because all of them were devout believers, or were economic necessity, and the possibility of previously unheard-of charity, more likely reasons for membership? The account certainly indicates ethnic rivalry as the cause of disagreement and jealousy. They were human – just like us!

Certainly those to whom 1 Peter is written 'are isolated little cells of Christians living within a vast civil society, and deprived of any support on the part of the authorities, or any friendship with the high and mighty'.[6] Such cells were made up of *paroikos* – people who were foreigners without citizenship, living away from home without civil rights and frequently beyond the protection of the law. It is from this word *paroika* that our word 'parish' comes, and it means 'the strangers who dwell alongside'.

At its best the parish church is a 'gathering of called out ones who, in the name of Jesus Christ, seek the welfare of the strangers who dwell alongside'. This understanding is potentially very exciting and reveals the possibility of rediscovering what the Church is and who it is for.

Part of the modern malaise in the Church is an obsession with its survival. So much emphasis is placed upon maintaining a particular culture, keeping things the way they are, ensuring the community is made up of 'people like us', and at all costs preventing change. One reason for this is because we have a static view of the gospel and of God. Subconsciously, if not consciously, there is a view that certain truths and doctrines come from God and, because God is the author of them, they are free of the influence of culture.

Peter recalls being at a conference in Singapore with a friend of his, a Brazilian bishop. The bishop wanted to buy a video camera. Peter tells how he and his friend visited many camera shops, and at each one the bishop asked how much the cameras were. Eventually, satisfied he had the best deal, the bishop bought a camera. A while later Peter visited him in Brazil. 'How is the camera?' he asked. 'It does not work,' replied his friend. 'It is not compatible.' Neither had thought about that while in Singapore! The question that should have been asked while purchasing the camera was 'Will it be compatible in Brazil?' Our gospel requires compatibility with the culture in which it is being shared. When we seek to share our faith we need to ask, 'How can it be received here?'

We may agree that the gospel can be stripped down to the basic truth that Jesus is Lord, but such a concept requires different interpretation in differing cultures. For example, the English concept of lordship, with its images of landed gentry and a political second chamber in government containing many unelected hereditary peers, needs considerable deconstructing if we are to understand the nature of Jesus' lordship in any relevant way. And such thinking needs to be repeated many times all over the world. For just as different video systems are necessary to translate pictures on camera into pictures on screen, so differences in culture require of the gospel considerable interpretation to different people, in different places and times.

## Weaving the tapestry

Broadwater Farm in North London is a late 60s/early 70s high density, slum-clearance concrete estate of high and low rise blocks, with about 3,500 residents. No church building was provided, so Christians had to go out of the estate for church services and for fellowship.

So where did this leave 'the church' here on the estate? After the riot in 1985 the repeated accusation from estate residents to the churches was: 'Where were you when we needed you?' There were three responses:

– Christians rushing in to preach to a deeply traumatized, wounded community.

- Christians preaching a spiritual gospel, unrelated to socio-political and justice issues.

- A lone, elderly nun moving into a flat on the estate just to be alongside people in their pain.

When that elderly nun moved on to the estate just after the riot, her witness was lonely and courageous. She moved out from the safety of her religious community to live on her own, in a flat, much the same as those around her, sharing their recent trauma and their devastation. Now there is a fellowship of people ...

We work together on pastoral and justice issues, involvement in the Community Health Centre. We challenge the statutory services when they fail the most vulnerable of our society. We celebrate, with hundreds of others, the huge diversity of God's people who live in our neighbourhood, at an annual multi-cultural carnival organized by one of our group. Some of us are involved with committees and the organization of the many activities and facets of the community . . . Whatever our personal and particular gifts and callings may be, all are complementary within the body of Christ here on the estate.

Out next planned programme is to invite the clergy and pastors of the surrounding churches to come with members of their congregations who live on the estate, to gather together to explore the questions:

> What does it mean to 'be church' here on Broadwater Farm Estate?

> What does it mean to 'be Christ' here on Broadwater Farm?

Frances Hawkey, *A Tapestry of Stories*

## So what is culture?

We need to understand what culture is. Culture is concerned with the way people behave and their customs; it has to do with the way people relate to each other through institutions such as marriage and law. Culture has to do with values in society and the world view of peoples.

Here are two perspectives on culture:

The first definition of culture, often called classicist, suggests that 'there is only one culture and it is universal and permanent'. Within this understanding of culture, one became 'cultured', and so listened to Bach and Beethoven, read Homer and Dickens and Flaubert, and appreciated Van Dyck, Michelango and Rembrandt. People of culture, in other words, nourished themselves on the great human achievements of the West.[7] And to this list of what made one cultured we might add the 1662 *Book of Common Prayer* and the Authorized Version of the Bible!

A second definition of culture, sometimes called empiricist, sees culture 'as a set of meanings and values that informs a way of life' – and there are obviously many such sets throughout the world. Within the parameters of this understanding of culture, one is 'cultured' by being socialized within a particular society. Culture is not something 'out there' but something that everyone participates in already.[8]

There are other cultures too – youth culture, internet and communications culture – all requiring different tools to unlock them. To understand the rock and pop culture, for example, requires some appreciation of the moral, social and peer pressures placed on people by role models such as pop stars, football players and other modern-day icons.

Culture determines how we do theology. If we view culture from the classicist perspective, then there can only be one theology, valid for all time, in all places and among all peoples. But if we view culture from an empiricist perspective, then 'not only can there be a theology for every culture and period of history, there must be'.[9] Theology becomes the tool by which religion makes sense in a particular culture, and theologians become the midwives of truth. To speak truth in today's youth culture, there needs to be an understanding of the pressures and mores that dominate and define that culture. Individualism plays a big part in such a culture, and often the way into it lies in encouraging individuality, but always seeking to push the boundaries towards community and concern for the other.

# What is gospel?

The heart of the gospel is that, out of love (Exodus 33.11; John 15.14-15), the invisible God (Colossians 1.15; 1 Timothy 1.17) is revealed in creation, through messengers and in person, making friends with human beings and living among them. The purpose of this is to invite and receive human beings into communion with God. In the person of Jesus Christ that God is most completely revealed, and through the Spirit of God the offer of friendship continues to be made to people in everyday life. That truth, however, is of little use unless people know how to receive such an offer of friendship and love. The challenge of theology in every time and place is to discern how the gift can be received within the outlook and values that inform people's daily living. This is an empiricist view of culture which we believe can enable us to speak truth in our time.

The word 'gospel' was originally associated with the propaganda of the Roman Empire. Literally it was news of a military victory on the far-flung frontiers of the Pax Romana or the accession to power of a new emperor. A 'gospel' was trumpeted as 'glad tidings' throughout the empire. The Emperor, Caesar, was eulogized as a 'divine man' on coins and in emperor cults.[10] The evangelist Mark uses the term 'gospel' (Mark 1.1; 1.15) to describe his literary genre about the decidedly non-imperial 'good news' about Jesus of Nazareth, a Jewish 'Christ'. Mark's excitement about Jesus' extraordinary life and witness leads him to invent a mode of writing that would go to the centre of the battle for hearts and minds which faced the ordinary people of his time.

This is the challenge that faces us. The popular media convey the gospel of our times, announcing propaganda of military, economic and spiritual victories near and far – victories that herald the power of the strong over the weak, the rich over the poor, the powerful over the powerless. New 'emperors' – whether they be computer software designers, media magnates, multinational companies, or amoral political leaders – have all mastered propaganda that speaks of new forms of divinity.

## Some conclusions

What we have said so far has a certain bias – a bias in favour of the view that following Jesus means being prepared to give our lives to make a difference where we live and work. The difference is the new order of Jesus, 'characterized by partnership, interdependence, equality of opportunity, and mutual respect that cuts across all distinctions between people'[11] – the realm of God. The spirit of this new order is love, born out of the God who comes in the person of Jesus to offer friendship and invite partnership, which heals society, offers peace, security, social justice and well-being, together with personal wholeness and the knowledge of God.

There is a bias here too about the Church, seeing it as a landing craft rather than an ark. We see the Church not so much as a place of safety and refuge, but rather as the community from which people are sent back into the world to reveal God's love. By returning to some of the roots of the early Church, we have tried to show that the primary purpose of those who gather in the name of Jesus Christ is not their own welfare, but the welfare of their neighbours – those who dwell alongside. Such living does not come cheap. We are invited to lay down our lives, not only for what we believe in and hope for, but through daily practice of the 'little virtues' that reflect a new order and make a difference.

# 3

# Taking practical steps

To make a difference it is essential to work together with others. The support of others is important and, more than that, community is integral to Christian faith. The gathering together of a small community was the first step for Jesus at the start of his public ministry. In this chapter we are going to look at practical steps in the development of small Christian communities – tried and tested steps taken by many such communities across the world.[1]

Small Christian communities are not house groups, although they often meet in people's homes and contain elements of such groups. They certainly study Scripture and pray. But they adopt and adapt ways of functioning that locate the focus of the group beyond itself, in the neighbourhood, the work-place, or place of learning.

Small Christian communities are supportive, even therapeutic, but that is incidental to their life rather than a primary function. They need resources for conflict resolution when differences occur over strategy, or when petty jealousies and rivalry threaten the life of the group. They are not heaven on earth and, like any human institution, they are made up of flawed individuals whose motives are as mixed, and lives as complex, as any other group. Such groups have their members who worry about whether 'people have paid', as in Dee Price's dream (see p. 4). Such 'payment' may be confusion over who has the 'right' to belong or a host of other things.

Small Christian communities are not better than other church, social or political groups, but they are often more focused. They can complement the wider Church and often exercise a prophetic function, but they also need the resources of the local church, as well as the insight, experience and resources of those whom

Robert Schreiter calls the 'professional theologians', more usually referred to as the priest, pastor or minister. Schreiter comments that he or she has 'an indispensable but limited role . . . the theologian helps to create the bonds of mutual accountability between the local and world church'.[2]

In Dee's dream there was a woman who did tricks. We can draw a parallel between her 'tricks' and the role of the small Christian community, whose works are often hidden, like the woman under the blanket; at other times the 'shape' of the group varies, depending on the function that it is called to perform at a given time. The terminology for such groups also varies from continent to continent. A friend who researched the terminology used for the growth of these small groups or communities listed over 3,000 different names or expressions. The list included titles such as small Christian community, small church community, basic ecclesial community and small faith community.[3] Some words appear frequently: small, basic, church, community. These words begin to answer our question: What is a small Christian community?

## Small

'Small' in this context means small enough to enable everyone to know each other and for the group to come together easily to share, yet big enough to make decisions and act together. Small could be ten or twelve people, but it could be as large as twenty to forty. Larger groups may include families and children who are also part of the community.

In our suggestions for building small Christian communities, we recognize that there are many church congregations of this size that have the potential to become such communities. Larger congregations could consider breaking down into smaller units, each a basic unit or cell of church.

## Basic

'Basic' here means having everyday concerns as its main focus, in particular what is essential or basic to living the Christian life.

One Catholic priest involved in such formation calls these 'groups for general living'.[4] They are made up of ordinary people from all walks of life. In this sense they are representative of the grassroots of society and have a particular concern for those regarded as insignificant, the hidden, voiceless ones, those who have been marginalized or suffered discrimination.

## Christian

The term 'Christian' is often applied to such communities, but so are the words 'eucharistic' and 'ecclesial'. In this context small Christian communities are more than ad hoc Christian groups. We are talking here of people coming together with the understanding that they are indeed 'church' in the sense that they are 'gathered' and have a concern for the welfare of their neighbourhood. They see the Eucharist or sharing of bread and wine (or in the case of Quakers, Salvationists and some Anabaptists the communal, sacramental life) as sustaining their wider witness. Their emphasis is on discovering what it means to be the people of God in a particular place and time.

## Community

Although we have been using the word 'group' alongside the word 'community', a distinction is necessary. A group often has a single focus, draws together people of a similar age, may only meet for a period of time and is often not a priority for its members. A community, by contrast, is concerned with the whole of life, draws together people of all ages, is likely to be long-term and is a priority for those who belong to it. Its development takes time and gives opportunity for a greater depth of relating.

A small Christian community is not merely a prayer or Bible study group, an extra to church life, or a few friends who enjoy each other's company. It has been described as

> the very foundation of church life, the place where we experience being part of the church. The point from which we go out in mission and the source of strength from which we bring the values of the gospel into the daily life of the neighbourhood.[5]

Such definitions are a touchstone for answering the question: What is a small Christian community? Because there are no look-alikes, there is no one correct definition. Each community has both a different starting point and a different objective. In this chapter we share practical steps that have helped in the ongoing formation of such communities the world over. Not all of these steps will be relevant all of the time, but they are tried and tested and therefore worth considering.

# How do we start?

Perhaps you have wished you could be part of such a community, or could start one. Or maybe you are already part of a small group, but the potential for becoming a small community has never really been considered. Decide first on what you are looking for, and then see if there are already such small Christian communities meeting locally. The local library might be able to provide you with this information, or the local council of churches. Other than this, approach one of the networks listed at the end of this book. Considering joining forces with others is always a good strategy. If you draw a blank here, then identify people who are asking similar questions or who seem to be on the same kind of faith journey as you – seeking to relate faith to life, or wanting to share their lives and concerns through taking action on issues of justice and lifestyle.

## Weaving the tapestry

Eight years ago, three of us living in Tiptree were involved in arranging a parish weekend, at which we welcomed the administrator of a theological seminary in the Philippines. What stayed with us was his obvious commitment to, love of, and strength that he gained from his Basic Christian Community. He spent a lot of his spare time working with the people who lived on the rubbish heaps – this was someone who took his faith to where people were.

So thinking about this the three of us started to meet, to try and thrash out how this could work for us in our locality. Over the years, more have joined us, some have left, some married, some become mothers; we are all still involved in our own local churches, two being vicars! We have all moved since we started and now live as far apart as Abingdon and Harwich! However, the commitment, strength, love and support for each other is there, and we continue to meet every two months for a whole day, to share where we are in life, to worship informally together and to reflect biblically on our experiences.

We are not a typical Basic Christian Community in the sense that we don't work together for transformation in any one locality, but we hope that we take back to our work wherever, shared principles of reality, biblical reflection, grassroots theology, a sharing of gifts and ministry. These, together with a vision of the coming of the kingdom of God for all, especially those who get lost in society and who are not heard, including those in our churches who have no voice.

Our name is 'Honkey-Tonk'. This comes from a lovely story brought by one of us about the way geese fly in formation. It is a story about shared effort in flight, care of the injured, sharing of the lead position, and what we all need to hear – 'honking' or encouragement as we fly.

Pauline Lamming, *A Tapestry of Stories*

A good place to start is by drawing a group of people together for a short period of time to see what is possible. Jeanne was recently with a group of seven women who came together like this just for a day; what happened was potentially one of those starting places. To build on such a starting place the group might then meet regularly for a period; no strings attached, just see what happens. If at the end of this time a collective decision is taken to continue, then building on that now becomes the responsibility of the whole group. The transition to corporate ownership is an important one.

Once this potential for groups of people to go further exists, all kinds of opportunities open up, more often than we realize. Again Jeanne has in mind a Lenten group to which she belonged. At the end, those who participated realized that they had travelled some way together and that there was the possibility of taking it further. The Lenten study had stirred vigorous debate about prisoners and in particular prisoners on Death Row. At one session the group watched a video of the film *Dead Man Walking*, a true story about one man awaiting execution. Deep personal feelings were touched on and shared, and at the end there was an expressed desire on the part of all in the group to take further a concern for prisoners – to know more, to visit a local prison. During this rather intense time, relationships had been forged and a concern had been identified, but other parochial demands prevailed. A parish course already scheduled took priority. Jeanne felt that an important opportunity had been missed; being 'open' to a new way will often mean being prepared to respond to the unexpected rather than following a more tried pattern.

## First steps

Founding a small Christian community can be a heady experience. With others you are building something new, something that might hold great promise for the future. Each person helps to shape it, bringing a unique contribution from his or her personal journey. As a group begins it needs to face:

- Who are we?
- What are we about?
- What is important to us?
- What are our gifts?
- What are our interests?

Some of this exploration may already have taken place in the weeks and months before. Once the decision to continue is made, the importance of these questions is heightened. Hearing each other's stories is the basis of a common identity. Stories are essential and time needs to be given to listen to each one. Knowing each other means getting beyond just the facts, so take your time. You do not have to share more than you feel safe about, but do share from the heart.

Small communities often focus on some common task or action, and taking time to get to know each other may sometimes be considered secondary. But the personal weaving together of each other's lives is at the heart of community, particularly when things get tough.

The sharing of personal stories creates a common or community identity. The questions listed above can help to clarify this common identity. Everyone needs to share the dream, and it is important to draw out everyone's responses. One way of doing this is to write down on pieces of card people's hopes and feelings for the project. One group doing this gathered up the cards and placed them face upwards on the floor. In the discussion that followed cards which did not represent the concerns of the group as a whole were turned over. The cards still facing upwards at the end of the exercise showed those on which all agreed. Everyone focused on these as they considered some next steps, and because all had participated equally in the process the next step became clearer.

## Naming

A name helps to forge a common identity. Choosing one is important, and deciding on a name can bring up all sorts of issues that it will be good to talk over. The process of choosing a name helps members to focus on their task and function. This can take time. One community that had difficulty deciding on a name just called itself the Thursday Group until eventually it settled on PATH – People at Home. One of the groups Peter belonged to was called One Step (see box on p. 26). The group was situated in a neighbourhood with many challenges. One Step symbolized the only way to face those challenges – 'one step at a time'. It also expressed a gospel truth that the most effective change happens 'one step at a time'.

## Agreeing what is important

Small communities need simple and flexible structures. By 'structures' we mean how often the group will meet, what they will do and how decisions will be made and by whom. Giving clear tasks to people helps to sharpen the focus and the sense of purpose or calling.

The folk who wrote their hopes and feelings down on pieces of card followed this exercise by asking themselves, 'What should we aim for in the next two years?' They then sorted the cards into three piles – essential, useful and bonus. Four aims emerged:

- We want to work with those who suffer deprivation, to learn from them and to develop their and our spirituality.

- We want to help people speak of their experiences – social, political, spiritual – in a liberating way.

- We want to work with people to effect change.

- We want to relate our work back to the institutional church.

These aims emerged, as one member put it, 'from this clarification exercise and umpteen other times when we prayed, reflected and teased things out together'.[6]

Once the purpose of the group is clear, agreeing about how often to meet, and when and where, will follow. This may seem obvious, but unless everyone involved knows exactly what has been agreed, and what they expect of each other, the small community may have a very short life indeed. Clear decisions and communications are essential for ongoing growth. So deciding how to communicate is an important decision to take early on. Recognize that not everyone will be able to come along every time, so there will be a need to keep in touch.

Be prepared for experimentation and change. By embarking on a process of community formation, you cannot know where the journey will end, or where it will take you. Being open to this reality keeps the community on its toes and helps its growth. Equally, journeys are not to be embarked on haphazardly either. Always ask, 'Why are we doing this now?'

## Weaving the tapestry

### One Step: Statement of purpose

The group which began meeting in May ... was a gathering of people from different churches living on the Jemima estate. The group was drawn together by members of the Fraternal, a body of people representing the Anglican, Roman Catholic, Methodist and Baptist Churches.

Most people living on Jemima have a feeling of 'passing through' and most feel there is nothing that they can do to change things. At one meeting one member spoke of how he just wanted to 'get out', but the thing that kept him there was that unless he and others worked for change, nothing would change.

As a group we are feeling our way to what it means to be a sign of change. The past few months have been like a parable that Jesus told of the seed growing secretly. The seed that has been hidden in the ground of the Jemima estate, a small insignificant group, has been hidden waiting for the nourishment from God in the earth of his love. The seed has begun to sprout, it is just showing above the surface. Still tender, still fragile – but still there.

The group, now called ONE STEP (One step at a time, sweet Jesus), exists to be a sign of hope and to make possible the kingdom life of God through service and biblical reflection. This is the way the kingdom is lived, ONE STEP at a time.

# More about structure

Small Christian communities need structure but not hierarchy. Integral to the effective management of such groups is the fact that each person has a place. Small Christian communities function best on the model of servanthood, where the group agrees to submit itself to the gift or function of a given member over a particular task or activity. However, this does not mean letting chaos reign, or allowing someone to use their gift or function as an occasion for 'throwing riding boots' at the group!

The world of jazz has something to offer here. One of the great jazz trumpeters, Wynton Marsalis, observed:

> In jazz you project your personality and discover positive and negative things about yourself. Because jazz is about projecting personality, and prizes individuality, it also puts responsibility upon you to figure out how to put your individuality in the context of a group . . . There is a lot of freedom in what we do, but the discipline is always there. And because in jazz you have to improvise, it is hard but necessary to maintain the discipline.[7]

Small church communities also 'prize individuality' but, as in jazz, 'within the context of the group'. To listen and submit oneself to the gift of another requires humility, trust and discipline.

Throughout the rest of this book we are going to be sharing 'tools' for small Christian communities – tools that are used the world over by those engaged in a new way of being church. We can think of them as certain tasks, functions or ministries that help a group to work well. We prefer the term ministries. The following list is not meant to be exclusive or exhaustive, but we have discovered that the things listed here are foundational to the effective development of a community.

- Welcome or hospitality
- Co-ordination
- Timekeeping
- Memory recollection

- Worship
- News sharing
- Biblical reflection
- Celebration or fiesta

# Ministries

## Welcome or hospitality

There are some people who have a way of making others feel welcome. As a group you will soon be able to identify such people. You will need somewhere to meet, so decide whose home or homes are best suited for this purpose. Sometimes it is good to have several bases, other times one or two are more convenient.

Practise hospitality, says St Paul. When we meet one another regularly it is easy to lose the courtesies and to take folk for granted. Each of us is fragile, and however robust we may appear on the surface, few of us can cope with being ignored, overlooked or neglected. Peter admits he has a deeply introverted side to his personality that is not easily seen. Some days, attending a group takes a lot of what his children called 'bottle'. In such fragile moments it is easy to get hurt or take offence, especially when none is intended. Good welcomers understand this and pay attention to the signs of vulnerability in both individuals and the group. Such people are invaluable.

In Africa there is a tradition known as Ubuntu – it is a way of describing community, and literally translated means 'I am because we are, and because we are, therefore I am'. In small Christian communities the focus is on the welfare of the other, particularly those within the neighbourhood or work-place. Group members may well encounter both hospitality and conflict in their efforts to do this work, and the group then becomes an essential place both of resource and refuge, enabling the work to go on.

Sharing meals is a good way of practising hospitality, but keep these simple and don't let them become an occasion for rivalry between group members. No one should feel excluded from the possibility of being a host, nor should the poorest members find it hard to bring something to a shared meal. At the same time, those who provide the welcome and hospitality should not be exploited, and the group will need to decide how to fund the comfort necessities of coffee, tea and biscuits!

Welcome is at the very heart of small Christian community life. A sacramental meal is, after all, central to Christian faith and practice; meals are referred to time and again throughout the gospels. It is therefore not surprising that Jesus took bread and wine to reveal his continuing presence among us. Nor perhaps is it surprising that many new ways of being church today are connected to coffee bars and restaurants. Jeanne, in her recent book *Changing Churches*, has suggested that 'café' might be a secular term which today could be applied to church, much as ecclesia applied in the early Church. Along with college and centre, she suggests – all places where people meet.

# 4

# Building community

'Communities have sometimes been referred to as leaderless groups. It is more accurate, however, to say that a community is a group where all are leaders.'[1] The matter of leadership in small Christian communities is crucial.

Scott Peck, who knew a lot about community, reflects on his experience in facilitating community formation: 'I have found that once a group becomes a community, my nominal job (as a designated leader) is over I can sit back and relax and be one among many, for another of the essential characteristics of community is a decentralization of authority.'[2]

## More ministries

In every community there are certain tasks or functions that need to be carried out. As well as the ministries listed at the end of the last chapter, we could include keeping accounts, writing letters, editing a newsletter – any number of jobs, depending on the purpose of the group. Let people volunteer for particular tasks; the jobs then get done and, more importantly, the underlying beliefs about sharing responsibility and organization are upheld.

In a small Christian community everyone needs to be equally responsible for the functioning of the group and the well-being of all its members. Anyone who takes on a task is taking it on, not as a position of status, but on behalf of all the members. It is easy to identify yourself with a particular role – 'I am the co-ordinator', 'I am the secretary', but primarily you are a member among members. Jeanne remembers hearing an elderly man – a Tanzanian – introduce himself at an international gathering as 'I am Christopher Mwoleka, a member of a small Christian community in Rulenge Diocese.' He was also the diocesan bishop and head of the delegation from Tanzania, but it was as a member of a small Christian community that he chose to introduce himself.

By seeing all positions as of equal value, one person is less likely to dominate the community and all members come to value themselves as individuals, as well as the gifts they have to bring. Recognizing the gifts that are present is important because different skills are likely to be needed at various times. Sometimes a simple group exercise can help, and Jeanne remembers a time in community when each member had a piece of card pinned to his or her back. She recalls:

> We then walked around and wrote on each other's cards what we valued about that person and the gifts that he or she contributed to the group. Once that was completed we sat in a circle and shared our responses to what other people had written. It was a deeply moving, affirming experience. For years after I carried my piece of card in the back of my diary, and I still have it today – worn and faint! It was also an exercise that helped us as community to recognize the gifts among us.

Holding lightly to positions does not mean thinking lightly of the particular skills that each member brings. Take, for example, the gift of making people feel welcome, or being good at throwing parties: those gifted in these ways can help others to gain similar skills; a sharing of responsibility develops; and the Christian community grows in maturity.

## The ministry of co-ordination

The Roman Catholic priest Jim O'Halloran, who has written extensively on community formation, speaks of co-ordinators rather than leaders, and says that it is good, where possible, to have a team of three. He says that there are practical and theological reasons for this: practically, there will be times when one person may have to be absent; and theologically, a team of co-ordinators maintains the principles of community even in the leadership. In his community such co-ordinators are chosen with care. A few meetings are devoted to the process, and consideration is given to the qualities needed at that particular time. After thought, particular people may be approached, 'Annette, would you mind?' 'Andrew, how about it?' Again, this is a matter of consensus, not of election. Co-ordinators then usually serve for a minimum of two years. Groups with only a small number of members might find this practice unworkable; but the principle is worth observing.[3]

Co-ordinating the group entails seeing that what needs to be done is done. Gaining consensus on decisions is an important, though often a difficult, thing to achieve, particularly if the community has come into existence through the vision and energy of one or two individuals who then need to share its ongoing development with others. But good co-ordinators try!

In our 'New Way of Being Church' course we emphasize the need for modelling a non-hierarchical way of working as church. We have had our difficulties over the years, and would have to admit to needing help in conflict resolution from time to time. But working through such conflict has been more than worthwhile.

In essence the task of co-ordination is to ensure that the elements listed are incorporated into the community's life. Co-ordination is about enabling the group to take responsibility for what it has undertaken to be and to do. Co-ordination is about the ability to organize, but perhaps more important, it is about gaining and keeping the confidence of the group and steering it gently in the agreed direction.

A co-ordinator's check-list will include

● making sure people know when and where to meet;

● ensuring that the other ministries are undertaken;

● arranging a schedule of activities with the timekeeper.

It is probably true to say that the bulk of the work of co-ordination is done outside the meetings, with a gentle eye kept on things.

# The ministry of timekeeping

This is a very practical ministry that can be undertaken by a member for just one meeting or for an agreed (short!) period of time. In New Way workshops we appoint timekeepers whose job it is to remind us when a session or exercise is due to end, and in particular to remind those of us who go on a bit that time is almost up! Few communities exist without a lot of meetings and talk, and overlong meetings or those dominated by a few longwinded people can become wearisome. Agreeing to a simple ground rule that one person will watch the time and help others to do the same makes all the difference. This is best kept separate from the job of chairing or co-ordinating. The timekeeper is not there to decide when the meeting will start or finish, but to give the signals.

Time is the only commodity which all human beings possess in equal measure. People who are busy need to know what they are committed to, and for how long. The prevailing wisdom is that people who are in executive jobs are most pressed for time. However, such people can often buy the help they need to make their lives more comfortable when they are free. Those who have two or three part-time, low-paid jobs to support life are just as busy, if not more so, and life is complicated by the need to find childminders and spend hard-earned money on convenience or fast food.

Many groups suffer from 'time lag' because questions like 'When shall we start and finish?' and 'How long shall we give to the different elements of the meeting?' have not been resolved. The timekeeper needs to work closely with the group co-ordinator in agreeing this process. If a meeting is scheduled to last one and a half hours, for example, time planning is essential. At the beginning of a group's life, people often feel uneasy about timekeeping, but as the tasks and vision of the group develop, the wisdom of time allocation becomes evident.

## The ministry of keeping the memory

Visiting small Christian communities in Latin America and parts of Africa, both of us are aware of the importance of recording memory and reciting the history of the community. Keeping a memory of meetings and events is not such a familiar practice here in Britain, but it is an important tool of community development. Keeping and recalling the memory provides a broad overall perspective. It is an encouragement in hard times and a call to ongoing commitment in easier times.

Groups whose vision is task oriented need to be reminded who they are and what they have done, as well as what they have agreed to do. Group memory is crucial to effective change. It is a written reminder of what the community has done and agreed. Those responsible for the memory should record the activities and insights of the group, as well as keeping notes on the decisions taken and actions proposed and accomplished. It is also helpful if the names and addresses of community members are recorded in the memory. The memory is not the minutes of the group; it is somewhere between a history and a check-list, and it only needs recording in a simple exercise book.

# Weaving the tapestry

## One Step: a sample 'memory'

*Present*: Jim, Ali, Ivor, Moira, etc.

We began with a reflection on the group's decision to ask Sue and Jim to write to the Council about the failure of the lights on the stairwell. No response yet. However, Jim said he'd met several people who'd sign a petition, and he'd heard someone had fallen in the dark.

Gospel tonight: 'you are the light of the world' – ironic cheers!

Stories: 'Who had lit the way for us?' Several spoke of teachers, youth workers. Genghis spoke of a Hindu friend who at Divali Hindu festival of light had given him a candle to celebrate their search for a better world.

'How can we be light?' Good question! This neighbourhood is bad at night. We discussed being available to help people when the lights failed – but couldn't yet think of a way of doing this. Talked about being lights for each other – by supporting one another better.

Reflection and action: Jim agreed to find out who had been hurt on the stairwell. We agreed to a petition and tried to see who else we could get involved.

Knock on the door around 8.30. Fred, who chairs the Housing Assn. He's depressed, no one comes to his meetings. He asks whether he can come to One Step. We talk about attending his next meeting too – raised with Fred the light issue.

Worship: You've guessed – it involves candles! Led by Ivor and Anne.

Next week: Bible reflection, etc.

In many groups the memory is shared every time they meet. It can be acted out, read as a poem, sung as a song, read verbatim … Be as creative as possible!

# Making decisions

Decision-making is essential to community life. Deciding by consensus is more appropriate than putting matters to a vote and helps to build up the group. In this way it is not a matter of those for and those against; by coming to a common mind or agreement, a decision is reached which is best for the community as a whole at that time. Opinions must be voiced, indeed they need to be, and this does not mean that there is never conflict or disagreement. Groups that are in it 'for real' will experience conflict from time to time. Learning something about conflict resolution is good. Consensus can and does work, and in the ordinary course of everyday life we make decisions by consensus much of the time. For a community this can take time, but it is time well spent.

Community-building skills are needed, such as listening, respecting others and speaking up.

*Listening*. In a discussion we are often thinking about what we want to say and when we can say it. But listening to what others are saying is a priority. We need to really listen to each other. Sometimes it is a good exercise to repeat what another person has just said. Listening is an art.

*Respecting*. Every person is to be respected. If I have difficulty listening, then it is worth asking myself, 'Do I respect this person?' Sometimes apparent lack of respect is because we have different personalities and deal with relationships differently. Try to deal quickly with blockages in relating to another, because not doing so can affect consensus decision-making and group solidarity.

*Speaking up*. In all communities there are those who say a lot and those who don't. In consensus decision-making it is essential that all have the opportunity to say what they think. Often it is those who say the least who have the key insights. Someone who thinks she is in a minority of one may prefer not to speak; instead she seems to consent to a decision and that inevitably rebounds later. If speaking up is essential, so is giving space for everyone to speak. A good co-ordinator will ensure that every voice is heard.

## Weaving the tapestry

The Neighbours is (a) community of households living in five adjoining terraced houses in a suburban road . . . The community was formed in 1984 and has a communal meeting room, utility room and large garden formed by knocking down four garden fences. There are eight adults, all lay people, and seven children. Traditions represented include Roman Catholic, Quaker and Anglican. They meet for prayers each morning, and regularly for meals and meetings, which include the children whenever possible. For some years the core activity was to offer accommodation to people recovering from mental illness, but this has diminished as the make-up of the community has changed. Members are supported in other activities such as a cooperative food business, a soup kitchen training for ordained ministry, work as a doctor and physiotherapist, organizing 'days of stillness'. A sustaining vision has been to seek a lifestyle which 'enables us to pray together daily, to do some things together and to support one another. The sort of community that can happen anywhere.'

Roger Sawtel, *A Tapestry of Stories*

*Seeking the common good.* The emphasis is on looking for the best answer for the community as a whole. Personal interests or preferences, though important, are not finally the issue. The core activity of the small Christian community is to seek the common good. A friend of ours shared recently about a decision that was being made in her group. She was the only one not in agreement. 'I told them', she said, 'that I was happy for them to go ahead, though I had my reservations. And I told them I would certainly support them in what they wanted to do.' However, there are occasions when someone may feel the need to withhold consent. When this happens, more 'standing back' may be necessary; it is important to listen to minorities.

Consensus decision-making requires listening and respect, and takes time. There is no perfect way to do anything. Nevertheless this way of making decisions works. Scott Peck says that in the many communities of which he has been a part, a thousand or more decisions have been made in this way. 'The process', he says, 'is itself an adventure . . . there is something inherently mystical about it.'[4] Jeanne comments that for a number of years now she has been part of a small working group in the village where she lives. There was no actual agreement to work by consensus, but that's what happens and it seems a natural way of working for a small group.

## Becoming friends

It is often a group of friends who come together to start a community. The challenge is to build on that and include others. It is one thing to start a venture with a friend or friends, it is quite another to get more deeply involved in each other's lives and include others. What may have seemed easy at first can prove to be quite difficult. In the 1970s Jeanne moved from London to Dorset to help found the Post Green Community. A few months after arriving at Post Green an awful thought struck her: 'Perhaps I won't like it in heaven either!' If we are expecting community-building to be easy, we are making a mistake. And the problem for us is most likely to be other people!

Scott Peck in *The Different Drum* reflects that when we start, all seems lovely – he calls this 'pseudo community'. He suggests that we then move on through chaos (trying to make the others into the people we want them to be) to emptiness (the temptation to give up) and then on to real community – accepting and living with differences.

This has certainly been our experience. Jeanne says that in the early days of the Post Green Community 'pseudo community' lasted but a short while, chaos a long time! She can remember during the latter period that she and Faith Lees, a close friend and co-founder, were eternally squabbling. It was wearying for both of them and for others too. One day a wise friend took them aside and suggested that it was differences in personality that caused the friction. 'You, Jeanne,' he told her, 'seem to need to get away and think through a matter before you do anything. You, Faith, need someone to talk with to help you come to a decision. Both of you are always expecting of the other what she cannot give.' His wise remarks about personality differences were way ahead of insights that are now more common knowledge, and they were spot on.

The closer people get to one another, the greater their expectations of one another, and close on the heels of such expectations comes the effort to change the other. Spouses and partners know all about this! Putting aside the desire to change the other is a difficult task. Understanding the other better helps. Sometimes self-discovery tools like the Myers Briggs Personality Indicator and the Enneagram can be useful, and it is worth investing some time in learning something about these methods of self-understanding.[5]

In the 1980s Peter and Jeanne were both part of a small team running a course in the Southwark Diocese. We ran into difficulties. We all liked each other as people, but group meetings were fraught with much heated argument and sometimes tears. The meetings went on far too long and tempers got even more frayed. Then we asked a friend who was a Myers Briggs consultant if she would help us. The understanding we gained from that changed the nature of our relating. Meetings more or less finished on time, and we enjoyed them.

We cannot emphasize enough that it takes time to build real community. There are no short cuts, but it can be infinitely worthwhile. And the building or nurturing never stops. Community can never be taken for granted, though this happens all too easily. One community in turmoil was faced with the decision of whether or not to continue. A consultant to the community advised them to stop meeting to deal with business and for six months to spend time renewing friendship. Immediately, members started making arrangements to have meals together and to go for walks; up to this point there had been little time for this. After a while the consultant had another suggestion. For a further period members formed pairs or groups of three that met to pray and share, but these pairs or trios changed every few weeks. In this way almost daily contact was maintained. It was a way of renewing friendship right across the community. In a community it is easy to bond with certain people and hardly to pass the time of day with others. Renewing friendship in this way helped this community to come to the decision to stay together.

Affirming one another is an important element of maintaining relationships. Affirmation can be expressed in many ways: a word, a note, a gift, an acknowledgement – even a smile! Community makes people vulnerable to each other. Vulnerability requires care and closeness, and can open up a healing experience for many. It is always an ongoing process.

# 5

# The whole of life

Worship is about giving worth to God. It is at the heart of community life. Here we recognize that the love which motivates us is a gift from the One whose love is for all, and for all time.

Include some simple act of worship in every group meeting. Creativity is called for because people may belong to different Christian traditions. A creative way of working with this can be for the community to begin to build its own ways of praying and worshipping together. Simple liturgies can be developed out of the sharing of everyday experiences, as well as the concerns and commitments that each holds. Sometimes simple objects brought from the home or just picked up in the street can provide symbols that focus sharing and prayer.

Jeanne recalls an occasion when each member of a group brought memorabilia of their early life – photographs, T-shirts, dolls, posters, books – a wonderful variety. Each person placed one object in the centre of the circle and explained its significance. The group then sat in silence for a while and reflected on all that had been brought – symbols of joy and struggle, despair and happiness. In closing, each person spoke of what had touched or challenged them. A simple liturgy that opened up the heart was created, and revealed one effective way of drawing people closer to God and one another.

## Further ministries

### The ministry of worship co-ordination

One of the important ministries in a small Christian community is that of worship co-ordinator or co-ordinators. Without co-ordination, worship can become perfunctory or static, or cease altogether. This is a task for those with imagination and sensitivity. The worship co-ordinator needs to be able to use the time available, often as little as a few minutes, to enable the group to reach beyond itself and experience something of the holy, something of God.

Here are some suggestions for worship co-ordination:

●     Agree with the group how much time will be allotted to worship at the meeting.

●     You may want to create a focal point to reflect the season of the year, or the life of the group, or both. In Advent, for example, candles and greenery on a seasonally coloured cloth spread over a coffee table or small table can provide a still point at the heart of a community meeting.

●     Keep worship simple. Sometimes a symbol like a broken brick, a piece of wire, a collection of autumn leaves or a bunch of spring flowers is as significant to the group's worship as candles, crosses and icons.

●     Be aware of occasions for celebration and commemoration. As well as religious seasons, there are personal and communal birthdays and anniversaries. And commemoration is important – remembering the loss of loved ones, or the anniversaries of those involved in significant struggles in the cause of justice, such as Martin Luther King, Mother Teresa, Dietrich Bonhoeffer, Pierre Gerety.[1]

Worship co-ordinators can keep in mind the possibilities and alert the group to them, while at the same time gathering suggestions from group members. Actual leadership of such simple acts of worship should rotate, most often with two, three or more people taking responsibility for an act of worship.

## Praying together

Praying together can take many forms. Sometimes it can be expressed through going for a walk in silence around a neighbourhood, noting what you see and then coming back and sharing what has caught your attention. This can lead to informed prayer. Or bring along cuttings from newspapers on events happening locally, nationally or internationally. Doing this will help you to bring local and world issues close and engage them with both heart and mind in prayer. At New Way workshops short summaries of current news are often brought to focus our mind in this way.

## Weaving the tapestry

We live in a time of change; perhaps it has always been that way. Like it or not, it is also a time of change in the Church. Some of us would like an unchanging church – Jesus Christ the same, yesterday, today and for ever. Some of us, feeling differently, decided, however, to explore another time of change, turbulence and uncertainty, seeing what we could learn for today. We took ourselves off to a weekend course to learn about Celtic spirituality at The Grail Community, just outside London, in Pinner, Middlesex.

After a day of learning about the Celts, how they lived and thought, our final day came when it was suggested that we make up our own Celtic service. We built a large Celtic cross of stones from the garden. It lay flat on the floor of the large round hall at The Grail. We decorated it with flowers and candles. It looked beautiful – an icon in itself. The Celtic style of worship was woven around the cross – prayers taken from various Celtic sources and some that we had written ourselves.

The attraction of this accessible prayer has grown with each of us since ... The Celts were concerned for their world, on which their livelihoods depended. We too recognize the need of being committed to the life of the planet. This involves life-style and choices in today's world, also choosing ways of living which are acceptable environmentally. Our prayer has made us turn outwards, away from personal concerns, to the needs of others, which are far greater.

Praying daily for world concerns is involving us in promoting attitudes of welcome and openness to those who are less well off. Celtic hospitality becomes a necessary part of our thinking, so we become involved with work for refugees, Jubilee 2000 as well as concern and care for our people locally. Occasionally we have a Celtic prayer workshop, which can take a whole day. Again this is something we do together, working out the form the services take, deciding on the theme, the movement or dance, considering the concerns of those who attend.

Anne Hope, *A Tapestry of Stories*

Small communities can become so immersed in immediate concerns that people forget the broader context in which these concerns are lived out. So prayer and worship need to be about the whole of life, growing out of life together. Don't forget to include these home-grown group liturgies in your community memory or journal. These will then become a valuable resource for your group's ongoing inner journey, that which undergirds its outer activity.

All of us have a need for times when we can express with others feelings that lie deep within. As Ann Morisy has put it:

Liturgy if it is to be apt needs to express people's deepest fears and hopes . . . Apt liturgy is a way of providing a framework of understanding which helps people to move beyond self centred and narrow horizons.[2]

Ann gives many examples in her book, *Beyond the Good Samaritan*, including an event that took place at the Jubilee Centre run by a Baptist church in South London. The centre's name came from the Old Testament, where it states that every 50 years God wanted the people of Israel to cancel all debts and give people a fresh start. The event was to mark the third birthday of the centre, and among those invited were many people who had approached the centre for help in rescheduling their debts.

Ann writes:

> The minister began by acknowledging everyone's debts to
> God for his gift of his Son. He asked God to forgive our
> society's preoccupation with material gain. He moved on
> to pray for those people who find themselves harassed by
> debt. He then prayed for the plight of nations in Africa and
> South America cast into debt through the world's system
> of commodity trading. One of the volunteers then read . . .
> about the time Jesus dined with Simon the Pharisee . . . the
> good guys in the story turned out to be a prostitute and the
> chap who owed the most money. Nobody preached, the
> short liturgy ended with the hymn 'The Servant King'.
> During the singing of the hymn there was scarcely a dry
> eye in the house.[3]

A simpler example comes from a New Way workshop. On arrival
at a conference centre we were told that we would have to move
from one room to another after the opening session. This was
unexpected and inconvenient. During the first session we seek to
build a sense of community, and this includes creating the right
atmosphere in the room, using various objects on a table, such as
a cloth, candles, etc. After some initial consternation we saw an
opportunity in the situation. We would have a simple liturgy of
moving place. When the evening meal was over we all gathered
in the first room and each took an object – the cross, the Bible, a
cloth, lighted candles, figures and stones, books, paper, pens. We
then processed silently to the second room, which meant going
outdoors and coming back in again, candles flickering. Inside,
standing in a circle, one after the other we spoke of how
unexpectedly moved we had been by this simple act. The
unplanned liturgy had in itself helped to create community.

Central to many of the small Christian communities that have
grown up in Latin America and elsewhere in the world is the
Eucharist or holy communion. Coming together to share bread
and wine can be a profound experience for any group. This is
something that many will want to include on a regular basis.
There may be difficulty when an ordained person is required to
officiate and there isn't one in the community. One solution is to

ask a priest or minister who is known to the community to come and celebrate. Having someone who is close to the group and sympathetic to its vision is essential. Some parish-based Anglican or Catholic communities are able to draw on the reserved sacrament, which can then be administered by lay persons.

An alternative is to have a simple breaking of bread – an agape. The Post Green Community decided on this option many years ago and has continued week in and week out to come together for an agape. Members of the community take it in turn to prepare a simple liturgy. At some point bread is broken and passed from person to person with words such as 'David, this is a sign of our common life', or 'Margaret, this is an expression of our love for each other'. Wine is also poured and a cup passed, with appropriate words spoken. However this is done, sharing bread and wine binds and holds a community together in a way that perhaps nothing else can.

Community prayer and worship can benefit from the many invaluable resources available. Those of Taizé and Iona are increasingly well known, and because they come out of community traditions can be an incentive to building one's own.

# News!

## The ministry of news

This sounds a bit like the Ministry of Agriculture, Food and Fisheries or a similar government department! Rather strange, perhaps, for a small Christian community, but ours is an age of news. This can be counter-productive at times, because news stories tend to get modified quite quickly. If news of a disaster begins to filter through, numbers are usually the first casualty of truth, either because they are too few or too many. But we seem to need news in our lives, perhaps because it keeps us in touch with life experiences other than our own. News can generate sympathy, anger, compassion and even action to bring about change.

We encourage a place for news in small Christian communities because it keeps us in touch with the real world. News can be brought to the community each time it meets – from the neighbourhood and the wider world. It can be both serious and light-hearted. To begin with, this activity may seem a little artificial, but it is worth persevering with, and in time its relevance to the group will become essential and vital. For this discipline to be integrated into the life of the community, someone needs to take responsibility for bringing items of news to share with the group. In New Way workshops we include news early on in the day so that it informs any prayer and Bible reading that may follow.

## Hearing the word of God today

Small church communities all around the world are rediscovering the Bible as a tool for everyday living. In this way hearing the word of God comes about when people read the Bible in the light of the everyday things that happen to them and to others, and as they meet in community.

Writing about the experience of a small Christian community on an estate in South London, Peter gives such an example:

> At some point in the evening someone would attempt to lead a reflection on a passage from the Bible that seemed to relate to the situation. For example, one evening people shared experiences of burglary. The group reflected on the gospel passages 'The thief comes only to break in and steal', 'If the householder had known when the burglar was coming he would have stayed awake' and 'I am come that you might have life in its fullness'. Someone asked, 'What would it means to have life in its fullness here?' The reply came, 'To live without fear of burglary and violence, a place of safety for the children', and so on. Someone then asked, 'Who would be Jesus here?' The reply came, 'We would have to be Jesus here.' Someone asked, 'What does it mean to stay awake?' The reply came, 'It means that we all share responsibility for making things different here.' Often as a result of its reflection the group would set itself a task.[4]

A diagram may help us explore this way of reading the Bible:

*Figure 1*

> One ear to the word
> One ear to the world
> Speak a word of God for our time

Because the criteria of community, Bible and reality are interrelated, they are moving towards a common objective – to listen to God today.

## The ministry of Bible reflection

Those responsible for this ministry in the group do not have to be theologians or biblical scholars. One of the decisions the group will need to make is how to use the Bible in its regular meetings. As we have said earlier, small church communities are not an alternative to the wider church, but complementary to it. Many churches follow a systematic reading of the Bible through the *Revised Common Lectionary*, which is used by many Anglicans, Roman Catholics and Methodists and covers the gospels over a period of three years. We have discovered that these passages are often surprisingly relevant if the group discusses the appropriate questions they raise.

There are many resources for groups; New Way Publications, for example, produces a series of studies based on the gospel readings in the *Revised Common Lectionary*. These are tailor-made for small church communities and consist of four parts:

- A reading from the gospel;

- An opportunity for people in the group to relate some experience of their own to the gospel;

- A brief comment on the gospel;

- A time of reflection in which questions are offered both for discussion and action; for example, someone might ask: Can anyone recall an example in the Bible that might speak to the situation we face?

However, reflecting on the Bible does not have to be so structured, and many of the most effective acts of biblical reflection occur almost spontaneously. During the early days of the conflict in Northern Ireland, for example, when the first tentative steps were being taken towards reconciling groups of people on both sides of the divide, one very effective yet simple method of biblical reflection was established. Each member of the group was asked to share a passage from the Bible that spoke to them, and say why it was so significant. This took place over several weeks, one or two people sharing an insight each week. What surprised the Protestant members of the group was that Catholics knew the same Bible stories as they did! Gradually confidence and trust were built up and led people eventually into the practicalities of peacemaking. What is often forgotten, when ceasefires and political agreements get signed, is that behind such mega-activity lies many years of micro-activity, with people working for reconciliation at grassroots level in small groups.

Because effective biblical reflection is something that we in these islands seem to find difficult, some further suggestions are given below in 'Weaving the tapestry'. The first is a simple process of looking at a Bible passage, seeing what it has to say to us in our situation, and then planning some action. The second example is a reflection on Matthew's Gospel, one of the 'set' gospels for the Church's year. By using set gospels, small groups can find ways of dovetailing their reflection and activities into the life of the wider Church.

## Weaving the tapestry

### Biblical reflection A

- After choosing a scripture passage, let someone read it aloud.

- Allow a few minutes of quiet personal reflection.

- Invite a brief sharing of thoughts – has anything spoken to us personally?

- Discuss whether anything in the passage speaks to the group about its work.

- Agree on any action that might be taken.

### Biblical reflection B

*Read the gospel*: Matthew 10.40-42. (Other readings: Genesis 22:1-14; Romans 6.12-23.)

*Story telling*: Share an experience of receiving unexpected hospitality.

*Comment*: Making people feel welcome and practising hospitality are the keys to living and working together as a small group. Matthew's churches were told to always expect the coming of Jesus, who said, 'I am with you always to the end of time.' 'In receiving the least of my brothers and sisters,' said Jesus, 'you receive me' (Matthew 25.20, 40). Making the least of the little ones, the just, the upright and the prophet feel at home is the same as making Jesus welcome.

Of course there are risks in such open hospitality. There are people who will take advantage, there will be those living among the just who are unjust. A prophet is someone who reads the signs of the times and challenges people to live their lives in a spirit of justice, peace and love before God and their neighbour. When a prophet's word is received and practised he (or she) has a prophet's reward (10.41). Similarly, where the example of someone living justly is followed by others, they too have the reward of a just person (10.41).

There can be no excuses about small groups failing to offer hospitality and welcome, because Jesus says if anyone gives so much as a cup of cold water . . . they will not go unrewarded (10.42). Hospitality, however simple, is a mark of justice, not charity. Christian living is not a matter of good intentions, but of justice: compassionate acts, listening to others or, more simply, fulfilling the law 'you shall love your neighbour as yourself'.

On the surface, giving cups of cold water, making strangers welcome and seeking to live in a just, peaceful and loving way would not seem to invite hostility and persecution. But Jesus, who lived his life this way (as we saw last week), attracted criticism and persecution.

*Reflection and action*: What can you as a group do to make people feel welcome among you? Are there situations where you can offer simple hospitality to people who are strangers or in some way left out in your community? What are the difficulties? How will you seek to overcome them? Pray – light a candle – say the Our Father – at 'give us this day our daily bread' pause and pray for those situations you have identified where you plan to practise hospitality – finish the prayer.

In the end, however, it is not particularly the process that matters; as our friend Angela wrote from the Philippines:

> Our attempts at being SCC groups have at least taken root. These are groups of people who meet together once a week to reflect on the Bible and see what relationship it has with their lives and see what action they need to take to better their situation. As a result they have grown very much in

their concern for each other and have bonded greatly as a group.

Writing about the impact of a recent typhoon on one of the neighbourhoods, when a 6-year-old boy was killed, Angela observed:

> The scriptures continue to come alive . . . because they spoke about God calling them to repentance and prayer. They acknowledged they were getting too caught up in trying to earn money, and perhaps were forgetting that God was very much a part of the chance they had been given to better themselves, and that the storm was a reminder to them not to forget the God who was with them, and was leading and protecting them. They seem to really understand what salvation history means.

Carlos Mesters has worked all his life among some of the most poverty-stricken and vulnerable people, for whom he has sought to develop relevant ways of reading the Bible and interpreting its message. He believes that the God who speaks today can be heard when the three factors of the Bible, the life of the community and people's daily reality are in dialogue with each other. It is his diagram we included earlier in this chapter.

## Weaving the tapestry

Why weren't they listening? It wasn't meant to be like this! I felt as if I really had something to say. I didn't feel I was boring. I'd spent my time over my sermon, address, call it what you will, but every week the same thing happened. People switched off. A nagging question preoccupied my thoughts. Was what I was saying irrelevant to these folk who had lived most of their lives on this run-down estate? Was my approach too middle-class? Did they want jokes? Perhaps I was simply inexperienced? What was going wrong?

After some time and prayer I realized that all of this was nothing to do with me, more to do with the method we use in our churches generally, a way of teaching which has been 'handed down' by generations of clergy. But this method, on the whole, disempowers our congregations from engaging with the Bible that they hear. The 'sermon' has become something which only the clergy or the lay readers comment on and interpret for the majority.

So, one Sunday morning, with my heart pounding in my chest I tried a different tactic. We read the reading and then the gospel. I had previously extracted a question which I thought I could throw out to the congregation for them to answer; an open ended question as opposed to one with a ready-made answer. After I had done so there was a long silence. A general atmosphere of people embarrassed at being put on the spot. Then slowly, tentatively, people began to speak. One or two at first and then several. I nicknamed my new method the 'dialogue sermon' and discovered much later that several clergy in Liverpool had been experimenting in the same way for the same reasons. After a few weeks I noticed that the congregation were generally more responsive.

One week, after a reading about the Widow's Mite, the theme I hoped to draw out was sacrifice. 'What does sacrifice mean for you?' I asked. A variety of people spoke and then there was a pause. I was about to continue when a voice I hadn't heard before spoke up. A woman, who sat with her disabled sister at the back of the church regularly Sunday after Sunday, was wanting to say something. I think I was the only person she spoke to usually, as she claimed she had fallen out with the rest of the congregation. I had often wondered why exactly she did come to church. But this Sunday was different.

'Sacrifice for me', Gilda said, 'has meant looking after Cathy here, my sister, all my life. Cathy fell down the stairs when she was quite young and hasn't been able to cope on her own ever since. None of my other family felt they could do this apart from me. I've never got married and I think it might be something to do with the way my life has been. Not that I mind or anything, this is just the way things are.'

After this speech, and on reflection afterwards, I thought how easy it is for those of us with the authority and supposed expertise to arrogantly assume that people do not understand or don't have anything to contribute in this way. I realize now that many people come to church, week after week, desperate to be able to share something like this, something of how their lives really are, and to be part of a group of people who will understand and support them.

Magdalen Smith, *A Tapestry of Stories*

'It doesn't matter so much', says Mesters,

from which of three aspects the process of interpretation is initiated, it depends on the circumstances, on history, on culture and the interests of the community or group. What matters is to notice that one aspect remains incomplete without the other two. In general, in all communities there are people who identify with one of the three aspects: people who want to know the Bible and are more interested in study; people who insist more on the community and its internal functions; and people who are concerned with serving people and in giving their contribution to political life and the social movement.[5]

Mesters was writing for a particular culture, and therefore his terminology requires some modification. But we can understand well enough the thrust of what he says. We all know people who are more tied up in the day-by-dayness of life's reality: those who look for political and social solutions, those who are good at making community work – peacemakers, reconcilers, conflict resolvers – and those who call us to prayer. What is perhaps not so common in our experience or understanding is how these different groups of people and situations need each other in order for us to hear God speak today. In church, if we are lucky, someone will have done a bit of homework on the Bible. He or she may draw out some profound truth that calls for a response in everyday life. Often, however, the predictable response is just 'Nice sermon, Vicar', as members of the congregation line up to shake hands at the door. An even more likely scenario is that the experiences of daily living are not taken into account at all by the preacher, and almost certainly no methodology is offered for taking this understanding out into the world.

We need a methodology – a praxis for making a difference.

# 6

# Making a difference

Small Christian communities exist to make a difference, to bring about change. If we are praying and worshipping and reading the Bible in the ways we have suggested, then one outcome will certainly be the desire to engage together in some form of action. How best to go about this is sometimes a question, and one tool that has helped many small Christian communities is the action/reflection or pastoral cycle.

## What is the pastoral cycle?

The pastoral cycle has a number of elements. The simplest cycle has three:

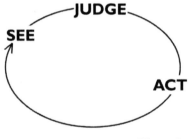

*Figure 2*

Here is an example of how this simple model might work. You are meeting as a group. One of your concerns is isolated single mums who are housebound. What you *see* is something you would like to change by helping to set up some short-term childcare, a babysitting service or something similar. What are the difficulties such an idea presents? Try to *judge* what the problems are. What needs to be done? Who can do it? When some of these problems have been addressed then comes the time for *action*.

The 'cycle' occurs when, having made some decisions and undertaken some action, the group revisits its agreed task to monitor its effectiveness. It is important to use this process as a 'cycle' to assess the ongoing effectiveness of the action.

There are different ways of working with this cycle. A Catholic Worker house in Oxford uses the model of prayer, study and action.

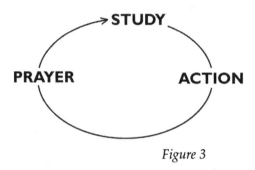

*Figure 3*

These Catholic Worker houses work for the welfare of the most vulnerable in our society, campaigning on issues of peace and justice. People who are committed to social action as their primary agenda often neglect spirituality. Prayer is not something we do to wake God up in the hope that we will get action. Prayer is the means by which God's hands are untied, because failure to pray somehow ties God's hands. This model of the pastoral cycle might be helpful for a group that meets in the first instance for prayer, but then wants to consider action, maybe as a result of studying the Bible or another book.

During the past years in New Way programmes, we have developed a pastoral cycle model which incorporates five elements:

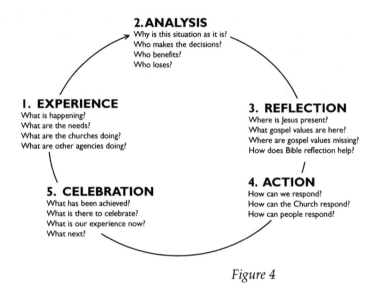

*Figure 4*

Ours is not a reflective society. We tend to look forward but seldom look back to discover what we have done. Some people say we are living in times that are 'strong on analysis, short on prescription'. By making use of a pastoral cycle we can find, if not prescriptions, at least the means of monitoring progress.

Sharon Welch, in *A Feminist Ethic of Risk*, asks the question: 'Why is it that white, middle-class, socially aware people often end up despairing over their lack of ability to effect changes in our socio-cultural, economic and religious institutions?'[1] She offers the following insights as to why this is so: educated, middle-class people want to see results. They tend to want social action to work according to the ideals and goals that motivate their actions. They measure their effectiveness by the criteria of their own ideas of success or failure. When failure rather than success is the end result of their impossible ideals and programmes, what Welch calls a 'cultured despair' sets in, and this is eventually following by a 'giving up'.

Sharon Welch observes that the luxury of despair and giving up is not an option among poor women in Africa, Asia and Latin

America particularly, where there are few, if any, guarantees about life and a 'given-ness', almost, that nothing will ever change. The ethic or guiding moral principle for such people is faithfulness, fidelity. This principle, rather than effectiveness, success or failure, 'creates a matrix in which further reflection, and a heritage of resistance and hope, becomes possible'.

'The biggest problem is keeping the vision alive,' commented a priest trying to build small church communities on an inner-city estate in Birmingham. Jeanne and other members of the New Way team were helping a group to work out the way ahead. Jeanne asked, 'How do you use the pastoral cycle?' The priest, who had attended a couple of New Way programmes, experienced one of those moments when light dawned. 'Well,' he responded, 'I have to admit we don't. But we should, shouldn't we? It's just that we keep on forgetting.'

## Using the pastoral cycle

There is a discipline involved here, but a worthwhile one. We break it down in the following way.

### Experience

Beginning with experience – our own story, the situation as we find it, the circumstances that surround us – we are able to begin the journey towards finding a way forward, healing the wounds, binding up the broken-hearted in our world.

### Analysis

Analysis is the most important, yet, next to celebration, the most neglected aspect of the pastoral cycle. Without adequate analysis we cannot make informed decisions on how to act, and action without analysis is often inappropriate and ultimately ineffective. The questions we ask often boil down to one simple one: Why? Why is this situation as it is? Why was it allowed to get this way? Why is no one doing anything about it? And so on.

## Weaving the tapestry

Some questions to help analyse situations in order to discover how to act:

- What are the major issues here?
- Why is this situation as it is?
- What are the most important causes of the way things are?

- Who makes the decisions round here?
- Who benefits?
- Who loses?

- Who has the power?
- What is the influence of money?
- What are the most important relationships?

- What needs to change?

- What has changed?
- What hasn't changed?

- If nothing changes, who will gain and who will lose?

By using some of the tools of social analysis we are able to discern why things are the way they are and can begin looking for solutions. Jesus often used questions as a way of enabling people to face their own powerlessness and to look for alternatives. Powerlessness often begins with fear. Jesus often asked, 'Why are you afraid?' 'What are you looking for?' 'What do you want to happen here?'

## Reflection

Reflecting on the answers we get to some of the questions we ask in our analysing process is important too. We need to 'check out' that we are hearing each other rightly. It is also an opportunity to discover that we are not the only people with concerns around here! Sometimes these others are people of religious faith, often not. When the group comes to reflect next time it meets, it will often observe, in answer to the question, 'Where are the gospel values present?', that there are other people who are seeking for justice, the welfare of the neighbourhood, reconciliation, conflict resolution and many other things besides.

## Action

Action is almost always a process of small steps. So it is important to remember that action is not only discovering how people can respond, but also seeing how we can involve ourselves or share with other people in responding. Doing something, however small, is often very satisfying, particularly if there has been good analytical preparation. However, it is not the action itself that matters as much as the way we observe things changing because of what we are doing.

## Celebration

Learning how to celebrate the small achievements is integral to the healthy life of the small Christian community. In our New Way workshops we always find time for celebration. Once we convened a gathering and neglected this aspect of our programme and one or two observant souls told us that they missed 'fiesta' – celebration – because of the way it lightened discussion or activity and restored energy.

We have found that food, sweets, simple dances, team games, 'Father Abraham' type songs and a host of other short and light activities make good occasions for celebration. Other events in the life of the community can be marked too, such as birthdays and anniversaries, particularly those that relate to the group. We often encourage people in areas where groups do not form easily to have a party once every three months or so to mark the continuance of the community. Celebration or fiesta is an occasion to be inventive. It's nearly always time for a party!

The pastoral cycle is a very simple but effective tool. The following story illustrates how using it worked for one community. It begins with 'a group of ordinary people in an ordinary town' – people from a number of different churches who came together to share their stories and an interest in an action/reflection way of doing theology.

This group started with the sharing of stories. Week by week people talked of their experiences, joys, pains and what living the Christian faith meant for them day by day. At this stage they didn't have much idea of what they were doing. However, they agreed that for each of them life was at times a bit of a struggle and were united in believing that despite this God made life worth living. There was also a common feeling that the Church was largely irrelevant to all of this.

From the sharing of stories a sense grew of what was lacking in the neighbourhood. Few facilities were available for people to meet socially and there was little sense of community. The group realized that it was not enough to take only their own experiences as evidence of what might be needed; they had to do some hard research. They now embarked on a new stage as they visited hundreds of homes and interviewed dozens of local groups and public services. For them this was engaging in mission. One member of the group says,

I'd always wondered why we always failed to do mission in Jesus' way. By the stories he told and the way he did things he always asked people questions, and I'd been trained always to have better and better answers.

Now their task was to go and ask questions and find out what people wanted. The answer was a neighbourhood centre.

A plan had emerged, but the group did not act on it immediately. Instead they 'went to the Bible'. They needed to prepare themselves for the journey ahead. They studied particular passages – Jeremiah's letters to the Jews in Babylonia, Jesus' teaching on prayer – but it was an underlying message that struck them, rather than any one story:

> the experience of struggle is a constant theme in the Bible which is often missed if we don't begin looking at the Bible from the personal struggles that we have. The word of God became the word of God for us – as a community.

This reassurance of God with them in the midst of struggle was to prove vital as the next steps were taken. The group was now ready to act, but they were only few in number and the task seemed overwhelming – thousands of pounds needed to be raised. They began to look round for a suitable building to refurbish, but found none. It was at this stage that they realized that their own church building could be adapted – an idea which had not been considered before and took them all by surprise. It was 'a scary thing' for all concerned. Nevertheless, within two years this is what happened and the neighbourhood centre was opened with a party and a service of thanksgiving. It has become a place for meeting and sharing life and faith.[2]

## Where the local church fits in

We have said earlier that small Christian communities are complementary to the wider Church. In Britain most small Christian communities exist alongside the local church, but in many parts of the world they are the Church at the most local level. There the local church itself is a small Christian community or, most often, a community of communities. In this case a local church may look rather like this:

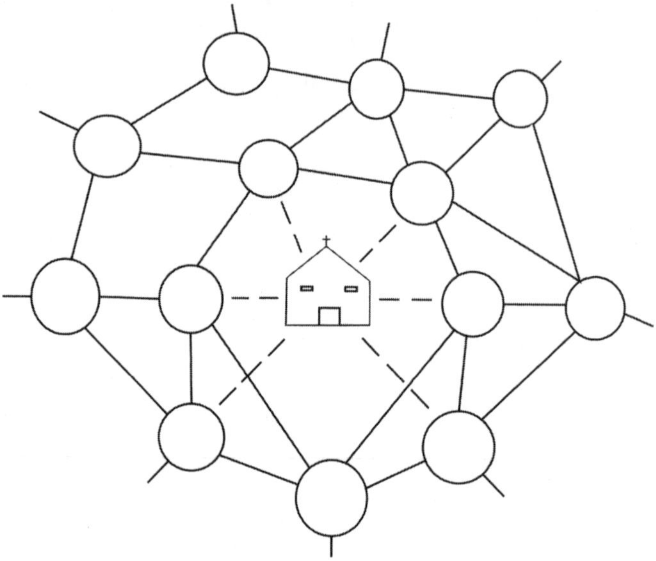

*Figure 5*

We are looking here at churches with congregations drawn from a wide area, numbering two or three thousand or more. Our churches are usually smaller than this! The New Way team has always encouraged local churches to move towards becoming such a community of communities or network of neighbourhood groups. For some local churches a first step might be to find ways to recognize and affirm the small communities that already exist in the locality. The Sunday liturgy can be a place where opportunity is given for sharing and reflection on the life and activity of these groups, but it takes planning and discipline to fit into the wider life of the eucharistic liturgy.

Once a local church has decided to restructure in favour of small Christian communities, the interactive processes of learning together can impact upon the whole life of the parish: the style of its liturgy, the nature of its gospel reflection and preaching, its committees and programmes – the whole bag. There are no short cuts to making a difference. However, few things are as rewarding as when a local church begins to experience its vocation in dwelling alongside and seeking the welfare of the neighbourhood.

## Weaving the tapestry

The conviction grew, borne out of many years of urban working class ministry, that there was something vital missing from the version of the gospel which we were proclaiming. There was an undeniable lack of connection between the 'theoretical good news' to which we were committed, and the concerns of most ordinary people in their everyday lives . . .

Following a workshop held in St Barnabas attended by a core of about 25 members there was a good deal of discussion about

- the development of the local church as a community of communities with a shift from congregation to the smaller group as the primary working unit of church;

- the change of orientation of the church from church programme to that of mission and the reign of God.

At the end of each preparation period we decided as a church community to take the process further. Up to that point home groups had been a basic feature of the life of the parish. There had been a sense of being a family together and this next stage was difficult. The basic strategy agreed was that the parish would be divided up into three or four geographical 'Mission Areas'. Each group was to be made up of members of the church who lived in each of the geographical areas, including children.

So in each of the three geographical areas there is a Neighbourhood Group whose primary purpose is mission in the widest sense. This local basic unit of church comes together to develop a reflective 'Jesus perspective' and share together the needs of the local area; to gain awareness of the people and situations they have encountered, and with a view to change towards the reign of God. This is 'mission' at the very simplest level and a real mobilization of the church at the grassroots. It involves evangelism, but it is much more than that; the agenda for the group is provided by 'life', the reality which surrounds us.

John Summers, *A Tapestry of Stories*

To sum up, there are three things integral to developing a methodology for making a difference.

● Small church/Christian communities.

● Creative interaction between these communities and the wider Church.

● Dynamic use of the pastoral cycle.

From our own experience we would say that every church member who takes the gospel imperative seriously should consider belonging to a small Christian community. These are workshops of transformation. Here healthy and fruitful tensions are experienced, shared and managed; here solutions are worked out and hope is ignited.

Small Christian communities are not house groups, although they may meet in houses. Some such communities may begin as house groups, but the purpose of a small Christian community is to be an agent of change, the means by which what is experienced in the daily realities of life, shared together in community and reflected upon in the light of the gospel, becomes the means whereby the Christian community shares in the process of transforming society.

Such groups become vital places of interactive learning, because here, through the process of listening to the stories and experiences of people, new options are opened up for gospel action. In this way they can be prophetic, pointing the way forward. Prophets are those who read the signs of the times and seek to interpret them through appropriate action. There may be times when tensions occur between the maintenance demands of the institutional Church and the more focused missiological task of the communities, but such tensions are creative and need not lead to breaking-point!

## Weaving the tapestry

**Differences between small groups and small communities[3]**

*Membership*: Homogeneous, tending towards uniformity; people of similar age, gender, specialization – e.g. youth, singles, marrieds, similar church tradition.

Pluralistic, bringing together peoples heterogeneous in age, social status, gender, religious commitment. Open, accessible to all, especially those with no say.

*Members' role*: Often just one of a person's many roles, e.g. leader.

Involves all aspects of the person; different sides of personality.

*Duration*: Temporary/ transitory; often linked to a specific task.

Long term: an expression of constant, stable, social life.

*Purpose*: Specialized, responding to one aspect / problem/task – such as praying, Bible study, social justice.

Broad, to be church together. Scripture/word. Eucharist/ ritual, mutuality, social engagement. Integrating fundamental dimensions of human life.

*Commitment*: Often for limited time – duration of season, programme or task.

Often unlimited or open ended. Task growing from commitment.

| | |
|---|---|
| *Dynamic*: Small group dynamic, often more satisfying to the articulate and those with group skills. | Community dynamic: open to a wider range of types of participation; may include small group activity. |
| *Intimacy*: Superficial but often intense. | Deeper/richer and usually slower in developing. |
| *Location*: Usually with a dependent part of a larger structure (e.g. a parish): does not aim for self-sufficiency: parish remains primary locus of belonging. | Ideally with a measure of self-sufficiency, but not cut off from wider church structures; networking is important; exists as the primary locus of belonging for the member. |

# The Sunday liturgy

In this model of a 'new way of being church' the parish continues to be seen as the primary expression of church life at the local level. Most parish structures are woefully inadequate for the restructuring of the parish into a 'community of small communities'. One writer presents the options clearly:

> Continue with the present structure of the parish and do lots of good programmes and outreach for the masses of parishioners, or re-structure the parish into small on going communities that are the Church at a small level while maintaining the parish community.[4]

As we have seen, as part of their life small Christian communities do study the Scriptures and pray. However, they seek to adopt and adapt to ways of working that place the focus of the group beyond itself, in the neighbourhood or work-place. Part of that focusing requires the community to apply the Bible to that reality. We need to explore processes whereby the neighbourhood experience of the small Christian community, and the wider Church interact and support each other. The clue to such interaction lies in the way the Bible, community and reality are brought to bear on one another, and how this is expressed and demonstrated in the Sunday liturgy.[5]

In New Way we believe that the role of the gathered congregation is integral to the success or otherwise of making the parish into a 'community of small communities'. At its heart is the ministry of the Word – preaching and teaching – which is the most undeveloped aspect of contemporary church life. Often it fails to relate to the daily life experiences of its hearers and the interaction between small Christian communities and the wider Church could be at its most creative in this area of Christian living.

Peter gives an illustration, based on experience. This puts in the wider parish context a story told earlier in the book.

> The church is set in the midst of an inner-city estate. It is attended by 30 or so people who are scattered around the church during the service. People sit more in ones than in twos, but there are a couple of families. The gospel reading for the day is from Luke 12 and contains the phrase 'if the householder had known what time the burglar would come, he would not have let anyone break through the wall of his house'. The preacher does not use the pulpit but comes down into the nave of the church and says: 'I've been burgled a number of times. I have lost most of the things that were precious and had sentimental value.' There is a pause. 'Has anyone here been burgled?' the preacher asks. Nearly everyone's hand goes up! The preacher moves among the congregation asking first one and then another what happened. Some speak of what they lost, others of how doors and windows were smashed.
>
> After a few minutes the preacher asks, 'Does anyone recall what the gospel reading was about?' One or two do. The preacher then asks whether Jesus said anything else about thieves and burglars. Someone recalls that he once said something about 'the thief only breaking in to steal and destroy', but that Jesus had said he had 'come so that people might have life to the full' (John 10.10). The question is then asked, 'What would it mean to "live life to the full" in the neighbourhood?' People reply that it would mean not being afraid of being burgled, mugged, or having drugs pushed. It would mean not having fears of violation or unwelcome invasion of privacy.

A discussion followed on the need for people to be more aware and alert for each other. Then the preacher asked, 'Who would be Jesus here?' Someone replied, 'It should be us. We are the ones who worship God and say it makes a difference.' The preacher asked, 'In the gospel of Luke it says that if he had known when the burglar was coming, the householder would have stayed awake. What does it mean to stay awake?' Someone replied that it would mean sharing responsibility for making things different here; another said that people needed to be more caring. 'What's preventing that?' asked the preacher. 'We do not know each other. We have to learn how to trust.'

That's where the sermon ended. But in the end, who was the preacher? In the local neighbourhood a small Christian community had been meeting for a few months. They too were reflecting on the gospel passage from Luke about the burgled household. Like the larger congregation, they shared their experiences of robbery and their sense of insecurity. During the months of the group meeting, a sense of trust had developed. People knew that the folk who were most likely to burgle them were their neighbours. The group had been trying to deal with another problem on the estate, an infestation of red ants. The pest control people had been slow to respond to the problem. The small Christian community had organized a petition, calling on people to demand action. Eventually, the operatives from the pest control came. They failed to gain access to the homes; people were at work, or out. Members of the group decided that someone would have to be trusted with the keys to people's flats if anything was to change. This was a big decision. People were having to risk that the trust they had built up really could be put to the test.

The following Sunday there was no visiting preacher. One of the members of the group had been there the previous Sunday. She offered to tell the story of their group and what they had learned, and tried to encourage the people to act on what they had discussed the previous Sunday. One or two did join the small Christian community.

Some months later a new minister came to the church and listened to the people's concerns about the estate. They told the minister about the sermon on burglary, and about the small group. At his first service the minister talked about the passage in Mark's gospel where Jesus describes himself as like a strong armed intruder who has come to 'tie up the strong man and take away his goods' (Mark 3.27). The minister asked if people were shocked to hear Jesus described as a burglar. They were! 'Why do you think Jesus described himself as someone who broke in and stole and tied up the householder?' People thought he wanted to shock his hearers. 'Why would Jesus want to do that?' asked the minister. 'Because he knew how strong his enemies were?' someone replied. 'Who were his enemies?' 'All those who opposed God by refusing to love and care for their neighbours,' said another. 'What do the followers of Jesus need to break in and steal? And who do they need to tie up?' asked the minister. 'We need to take action on behalf of those on this estate who are afraid,' came the reply.

And so the story goes on! Lest readers should be misled, in each of the gospel discussions the preacher and the minister had both prepared very thoroughly beforehand, but with sufficient flexibility in both the questions they asked and the exegesis they might give, depending on the response from the congregation. And, as the illustration shows, it doesn't matter whether the starting point is living in the community, feeling the reality, or respecting the biblical text.

# Constructing local theology

Robert Schreiter, in his book *Constructing Local Theologies*, speaks of the pastor, minister or parish priest as ideally fulfilling the role of the professional theologian in the community. 'Being a theologian is a gift requiring a sensitivity to the context, an extraordinary capacity to listen, and an immersion in the Scriptures,' he writes.[6] If the ministry of the Word on a Sunday is to have any cash value during the week, then sensitivity to (local) context and that most un-clerical virtue, an extraordinary capacity to listen to the community, must both inform and be informed by an immersion in the Scriptures. In such a situation it is possible to develop what Schreiter calls local theology, whose 'principal roots are gospel, Church and culture'.[7]

We need to be honest here: much of the professional theologian's training, with its emphasis on immersion in Scripture and the role and place of the study in the minister's house, leads to a separation from, rather than an engagement with, the experience of those living in the community. Often there is little ability to relate theology in down-to-earth terms to those for whom it is intended; namely, the community itself. Too often we fail to allow for the fact that God, who is the source of our theology, is already at work in communities, neighbourhoods and work-places and among believers and unbelievers alike! The important thing is to find ways of enabling reflection on the gospel to include the experience and insights of people who for the most part do not believe themselves to be theologically able.

Peter recalls that after the horrendous bombing of the town of Omagh in Northern Ireland in August 1998, he and Dee attended the Memorial Service in the town centre. Standing with them was a man who had lost his wife in the bombing. 'I don't bother God much,' he observed, 'and I was dreading the day I buried my wife. I asked God to help. As her body was lowered into the ground, I experienced such an inner strength that I knew it was not my own.' Peter comments, 'Dee and I had been sent to support and comfort. He knew a greater comfort!'

Schreiter is right, of course, when he says, 'Not everything that any community says or does can be called theology.' But he is equally correct when he asserts that 'theology is certainly intended for the community and is not meant to remain the property of a theologian class. The expression of faith in theology should make a difference in people's lives; otherwise it is a mere beating of the air. Reflection for its own sake may lead to contemplation, but contemplation should lead to action as well.'

# Five loaves and two fishes

The story of the feeding of the five thousand (Matthew 14.13-21) well illustrates the points made in this chapter.

At this point in his ministry Jesus is confronted with overwhelming challenges. First, he is personally in considerable political danger. His cousin and mentor John has been executed in the dungeons of Herod's fortress. Secondly, he has been facing the hostility and indifference of the religious authorities to his message of liberation. Thirdly, it has been a long day in the desert with the disaffected, landless and hungry poor. Recognizing their hunger, Jesus tells his disciples to respond to their need rather than seek to get rid of them.

Resources are sought within the crowd, and what is immediately forthcoming is distinctly limited – five loaves and two fish! Taking what is offered, Jesus seeks God's blessing, and the situation is transformed and a solution found. It is a solution that meets the need of the people in the most pastorally appropriate way – and there is a surplus.

The story is both parable and miracle. Jesus has been moved by the plight of the people and his response to them is born out of that compassion. In essence that is the energy needed to drive God's people, who also face overwhelming challenges today. When we face situations that we know need changing and sense that a response is demanded of us, the first challenge is to assess what resources are available locally. Like the response in the gospel, we may find that these resources are extremely limited. What motivates the people of God is the conviction that God has the power to transform situations, but we should note that the activity of transformation followed on from the recognition of need and the willingness to respond by seeking the resources available. Solutions do not fall into our lap – but they do come!

# 7

# A new way of
# being local church

Small Christian communities are a sign of the reign of God, leaven in the lump. They are not an end in themselves. They point to a future waiting to be born. They are a sign of hope and, as one T-shirt slogan reminds us, 'Hope is believing in spite of the evidence, and watching the evidence change'.

Each year, just before the season of Advent, we celebrate the feast of Christ the King. Although it is close to the Christmas season, the readings in the Anglican lectionary are Luke's account of Jesus' crucifixion, which gives a more sober and real backdrop to the approaching festivities. The coronation of Jesus is a cross. His rule begins in suffering, both for, with and among his people. Celebrating Christ's alternative kingship at this time in the year reminds his would-be followers of the nature of the life to which they are commited. Crucifixion as a form of judicial execution was reserved for revolutionaries and slaves. In what way did the Jewish authorities perceive Jesus as a revolutionary – or, at the very least, a threat to the *status quo* – who deserved to die?

His values, his concern for the poor, his recognition of women, including his willingness to have women who were unrelated to him travelling with his party, seem innocuous enough. We know that he lived simply and sparingly and was strongly against holding on to surplus goods. His criticism of the rich for failing to sell their surplus possessions to share with the poor and hungry inevitably brought him hostility. Jesus' teaching was certainly potentially disruptive, and he challenged the existing social order because it was based upon domination and violence. His own rejection of violence and his criticism of those who dominated their subjects was brave and consistent. Jesus refused to co-operate with, or defer to, any authority that did not accord with the patterns of behaviour desired by God.

Jesus' witness to others was marked by a spirit of humility and service. He looked in vain for similar responses from the religious leaders of his time. He described the religious hegemony harshly as 'wicked tenants' and 'whitewashed tombs' and would turn their frequent questions on themselves, refusing to answer when he discerned he would not be taken seriously.

Jesus' refusal to conform to existing social patterns or to be intimidated by the powerful and their henchmen and his championing of the poor, vulnerable and marginalized meant that, while he may not have been a direct threat to the establishment, he certainly put it on notice. No oppressive structure could ultimately stand against such determination.

It is Jesus, then, who provides us with the vision of resistance and hope for the future. The small Christian community is perhaps the most significant and creative sign of hope for the future of the Church.

## In for the long haul

Our commitment to the struggle to build small Christian communities is thus born out of a passionate conviction that the gospel of Jesus Christ is about building a world of truth, justice and harmony shaped by self-giving love. But it is tough going, and we often pack it in because we do not know how to keep going in the struggle. In an article in *Sojourners* Walter Wink put it like this: 'We are not easily reduced to prayer. We who grope towards praying today are like a city gutted by fire. The struggle against injustice has exacted from us an awful cost.'[1] In a similar though earlier period, the French existentialist philosopher Albert Camus wrote:

> There is merely bad luck in not being loved; there is tragedy in not loving. All of us today are dying of the tragedy. For violence and hatred dry up the heart itself; the long fight for justice exhausts the love that nevertheless

gave birth to it. In the clamour in which we live, love is impossible and justice does not suffice.'[2]

Sharon Welch writes: 'A true ethic of risk retains commitment even, and especially, in the face of uncertainty, the lack of a guarantee and the knowledge that things may never change.'[3]

Often the struggle is found in working out relationships within the group itself. Ideas about modelling 'the church of the future' are heady stuff, but what about real life when you can't get on with someone, where you can't agree as a group, where a piece of action has grossly misfired or one member has scarpered with the CD player? Difficulties have to be faced. They are part of reality. Perhaps the community has become a target of misinformation, is misunderstood by others, or under attack perhaps by some who have left the group. This kind of thing happened in the early Church too and has happened in the history of the Church ever since. Small Christian communities are formed in the daily realities of real life and will often reflect this in many uncomfortable and embarrassing ways. The early Church communities mirrored all the problems of their time, and the New Testament witnesses to their day-to-day struggle to live a gospel lifestyle within these situations. It is in such situations that gospel words like 'justice', 'forgiveness' and 'reconciliation' take on a new edge.

Small groups benefit enormously from a wise person who will accompany the community as a soul friend or consultant. This should be someone to whom individuals can talk and who is there for the whole community, someone who is a companion walking alongside, not making decisions but at times facilitating the community in its decision making. Many communities have a 'wise friend' or consultant, who visits two or three times a year and is available in a crisis.

# A personal struggle

Sometimes the struggle is a more personal one, because there are no others to link up with, or so it seems, anyway. But there are still choices that can be made. Carol Stickland's situation was a bit like this and she tells it this way:

> My husband and I, with our two small children, moved to a new town, and as we firmly believed we should worship in our local community, we joined the parish church. We heard lots of sermons about the need to change, and the PCC was restructured into groups, one of which discussed 'mission'. All looked hopeful, but as time went by it became obvious that there was no real willingness to change anything This parish felt that 'church' meant doing services, the same structure each week. Frustration set in!
>
> At this point we were encouraged by a friend to attend a series of workshops under the title 'New Way of Being Church'. The concepts we discovered were really exciting and so, full of enthusiasm, we went back to our parish. We asked if we could give a brief report back to the PCC and then handed invitations to each member to supper and a taster workshop in our home. The invitation was tendered to the whole congregation. Four people came (from a congregation of 100+) and they enjoyed the evening, but as the clergy were not interested we were unable to move on as a parish.
>
> We reluctantly decided that we could no longer remain in a church that had so little interest in the world beyond its doors. I was surprised just how much it hurt me to give up on a church, and many tears were shed before we settled into the local Methodist church. This was a very busy church, the sort where, if you wished to, you could be at events or meetings every day and evening. We had to work out our priorities, so I told one of the church leaders that I would only join in with 'activities' that involved people who *didn't* come to church and that served the community. In some churches that would leave you with a very quiet life!
>
> A few months down the line I was asked to run the 'Parents and Toddlers' group. I was impressed, because I was supported in the work. From the beginning the mums

have been impressed with the number of adults we provide for the crèche, a much better adult/child ratio than in a leisure centre. Health visitors in our town send new people to us and parents tell other parents. We have now reached the point that we have two sessions a week to cope with the numbers. At church festival times we have relevant activities, including the noisiest Carol Service you have ever experienced!

In the summer we have a toddler party which needs lots of space, and as we have no outdoor area I tentatively asked if we could use the church as well as the hall. This was accepted, and so I really tested people's tolerance by putting up a bouncy castle in the church. The church was the safest place as it was carpeted and enclosed. The only problem I encountered with the congregation was getting one of the church stewards to finish his turn on the bouncy castle![4]

## Training for mission

Implied in much that has been said in this book is the need for change in the institutional Church. This is not a particularly surprising statement; much has been written about the need for it. Perhaps there is less agreement over what needs to change. Peter comments on one post-ordination training programme he was asked to approve. He considered that it had many excellent elements, but what he saw as obviously missing was anything about community building, community development and organizing, or conflict resolution. Nor was there any reference to seeking the welfare of the poor and excluded in our society. There were general references to evangelism, and to a variety of ready-made courses, but no methodology for understanding the culture in which people are called to ministry or encouragement to experiment. Consideration of issues such as human relations, communication skills, commitment to justice and evidence of ability to work with, and help build up, the local community apart from the church was simply not required.

In researching *Changing Churches*, Jeanne became aware of another kind of gap – that between lay and ordained. There seemed to be very little relevant training to enable lay people to *be* the church, to engage in the task of ministry as church in the world. The Churches' Commission on Mission/Building Bridges of Hope Data Analysis backs this up when it states:

> There has been very little response to the question, 'What people development is consciously taking place?' Most training is of a general nature, and is not focused on how to deal with local practicalities. The data shows that the development of laity and clergy is mainly separate even though they are required to work together locally.[5]

Perhaps more stark was the number of newly trained ministers who did not survive even one year in their new appointments.

If small Christian communities are to grow within local churches – as a new way of being church – then new forms of ministry and training also need to be encouraged. The phrase 'a new way of being local church' is the one most used of the small Christian communities in East Africa. Small Christian communities are not an addition to the Church, they *are* the Church. In her report on visits made to small Christian communities in East Africa in Spring 2002, Jeanne shares a conversation with the parish priest of a Catholic parish in Nairobi, Kenya:

> The parish priest, Fr John Wamuti, at Holy Trinity Church, was away most of my visit but we met briefly just before I left. 'Small Christian communities have been written about as "the shape of the future church",' I said to him. 'Here in East Africa it seems in many places that shape has already arrived. But will it last? Have the communities a future still?'
>
> 'Oh, most certainly,' came the immediate, almost surprised, response. He continued, 'It is the church that makes sense to ordinary people. It is what they want. It is what they live out themselves.'
>
> I knew that there had been small Christian communities in the parish before John came to it, and so I asked: 'Was it

difficult to come into a parish that was already shaped in this way? Did you feel you couldn't change anything?'

Again he seemed surprised at my question.

'I see my job as a parish priest is to serve this church. This means to support what has developed in whatever ways are helpful and appropriate. The people of this parish will be here when I have moved on; they are the church here.'[6]

# Networking

We have written several times of the importance of facilitation in the ongoing life of a small Christian community, and the role of the minister as facilitator may be key here. Another way of both giving and receiving support is through networking. An important step therefore is to find out what allies there are in the wider community, say within a 50 mile radius. By allies we mean other small Christian communities, justice and peace networks and community groups. Some may not be overtly Christian, indeed some may be of other faiths. There may already be networks in place which you can join if appropriate, or your small Christian community may be the catalyst to bring this about.

In the late 1950s Jeanne was part of an informal network of open youth clubs across London. At a conference on open youth work the decision was taken by some to start meeting together on a regular basis for mutual support. This continued for some years and there was interaction too among the clubs as time went on. Gradually other steps were taken and the informal network became the Frontier Youth Trust, an organization challenging traditional ways of Christian youth work and, indeed, modelling another way of being church – for young people. Such networks and grassroots movements are an important way of moving things forward.

It is important to let others know you exist! Also, as you consider different kinds of action, find out first if others are doing something similar and find ways of supporting or adding to that initiative rather than duplicating it. This is an important way of helping to build social capital in local communities.

# A final ministry: Fiesta

Networking gatherings are often a time for partying. In the Latin American communities they use the word *fiesta*. Whether with others or on their own, a small Christian community will quickly realize the importance of this *ministry of fiesta*. Often what is celebrated are achievements, even little ones – reasons for gratitude. Sometimes when there is nothing to celebrate, the one thing to do is celebrate! Celebration can be as simple as passing round a bar of chocolate – albeit with style.

This is an essential aspect of New Way workshops. Some kind of fiesta takes place at every session. One or two people take responsibility for this ministry, which we consider so essential that New Way has produced a small booklet devoted to it: *Celebration: Fiesta Fun for Small Christian Communities* by Magdalen Smith. In it Magdalen writes:

> In small Christian communities all over the world the idea of celebration – or fiesta – is threaded in and through life and is itself part of what is called the Pastoral Cycle. In other words, fiesta is not an optional extra to be fitted in only if there is time, but speaks of the more profound realities of the experience of celebration in a shared community. Fiesta becomes all the more meaningful when people know one another and have shared something of their lives together at different points. In 1999 I travelled to Bolivia, in South America, to participate in an international conference on small Christian communities. As part of the week spent there participants representing different areas of the world were asked to organize fiestas as part of the time people spend relaxing together. The fiesta took the form of 'celebrations of life'. These were illustrations of how people might celebrate in two particular areas of the world, North America and Oceania. The first, Oceania, comprised representatives from Australia and Papua New Guinea. Activities included conch-shell blowing – an activity used to call people to worship in some of the islands – and didgeridoo playing from Australia. Much

laughter was had as volunteers practised air control by first blowing air into a glass of water through a straw.

North America's 'celebration' was made up of line-dancing, charades, and then the creating and eating of crackers, chocolate and marshmallows around a camp-fire – apparently a traditional snack eaten by young people as they venture off to summer camp! Both of these 'celebrations of life' proved a wonderful way for people to have fun together. As well as understanding something about different cultures.[7]

# Marking the milestones

Communities quickly begin to gather to themselves traditions: ways of doing things, celebrating anniversaries, welcoming new members, saying goodbye. All these are important to family life and to the community. They are also important components of building community.

Sometimes a milestone marks an ending. When people leave, for whatever reason, it is a sad moment; often words are inadequate to express feelings and a simple liturgy can help at times like these. Community liturgies can be important moments at other times too – a bereavement, a crisis, or a reconciliation. Using symbols that can be simply explained may be an opportunity to express in a few words what would otherwise be difficult to say. Silence, readings, movement, the lighting of candles, the offering of gifts, can be included in ways that allow for expressions of joy, sorrow, grief, anger or laughter.

Communities also end. Some have a long lifespan, some a short one. In our mobile society, many communities exist only for a short period. In all, change is constant. The story is always needing to be updated. The stories told in this book are of a period in time. The experiences shared nevertheless continue to encourage and inform us.

It is not the length of time that a community exists that is important. What matters is what endures and the effect it has on the lives of all involved and on others around. Community changes people: from our experience, we would say it marks people for life We mean that in a good way. Those who have been part of a community are likely to want to build community wherever they find themselves. And given the nature of our society, some of us may belong to several small Christian communities in our lifetime.

We need to bear in mind that we are part of a larger picture. Change usually happens very gradually, bit by bit, piece by piece, and in the meantime we often see only our own little contribution and that of others struggling against the odds. As we remain faithful to our understanding of God's vision for the future, we begin to see what we are about as part of a bigger plan.

Small Christian communities seek to bring about change from below – from the grassroots. They seek a restructuring of the Church so that it is more relevant, particularly to those on the outside. As agents for change, they model the shape of the coming Church. A Franciscan priest puts it this way: 'Today's basic communities hold a prophecy, a promise that is slowly becoming historical reality. We shall have a new church, a church born of the faith that nourishes God's people.'[8]

# Notes

## Introduction

1    The Iona hymn is copyright © 1989, Wild Goose Resource Group, Iona Community, Glasgow, Scotland. Reproduced by permission.

## 1  Flowers along the path

1    Michael Bridgwater, New Way newsletter, Spring 1998.

2    Case Study, Peter Price, 1991.

3    Case Study, Doorway, 1991.

## 2  What is church?

1    Recounted in Peter B. Price, *The Church as Kingdom – A New Way of Being Church* (Marshall Pickering, 1987).

2    The outcome of these discussions was produced a while later in *God, Jesus and You – First Steps in Faith* (Bible Society, 1979).

3    This list of 'little virtues' has been adapted from those offered by Eduardo Hoornaert in his brilliant book on the first Christian communities, *Memory of the Christian People* (Burns and Oates, 1989).

4    Hoornaert, *Memory*, p. 32.

5    See Jeanne Hinton, *Changing Churches: Building Bridges in Local Mission* (CTBI, 2001), pp. 102–6.

6    Hoornaert, *Memory*, where he develops the issue of the Christian community as both 'organized social protest, a line of defence against the social atomization that posed such a threat to these landless folk who had to live without rights, without a particular trade, and without protection' (p. 32) and as 'communities which appeared closed, isolated and secret in their own life . . . experiencing a "new land and a new sky where justice abides" (2 Peter 3.13), a new Exodus: "Our dwelling is in heaven" (Philippians 3.20)'.

7    For a fuller development of this thinking see Stephen B. Bevans, *Models of Contextual Theology* (Orbis, 1992).

8    Bevans, *Models*, p. 7. This definition can also be found in Bernard Lonergan, *Method in Theology*.

9    Bevans, *Models*, p. 7.

10    Ched Myers et al., edited Karen Lattea: *Say to this Mountain: Mark's Story of Discipleship* (Orbis, 1996), pp. 5–6.

11   Walter Wink, *Engaging the Powers* (Fortress, 1992). Wink speaks of God's reign as a 'domination free order characterized by partnership, interdependence and equality of opportunity, and mutual respect between men and women that cuts across all distinctions between people' (p.107).

## 3   Taking practical steps

1   Small Christian communities are, by their nature, self-defining. This is an inconvenient fact for demographers and for those who prefer their reality to be tidy and readily categorizable. But the authors believe that, looking both at the examples they have given in this book and the categories explained in this section, it will be quite possible for readers to work out what does and does not constitute an appropriate understanding of 'small Christian community' in their context. As Ian Fraser's recent collection (*Reinventing Church*, Iona Community, 2001) emphasizes, the definition will in any case evolve as the expression of 'small Christian community' evolves to meet new challenges and answer new questions.

2   Robert Schreiter, *Constructing Local Theologies* (Orbis, 1985), pp. 17–18.

3   Joseph Healey, Background Paper for Consultation on 'Rediscovering Community', Notre Dame, USA, 1991.

4   Case Study, Jeanne Hinton, 1995.

5   Case Study, Jeanne Hinton, 1995.

6   Case Study, Doorway, 1991.

7   Wynton Marsalis on London Weekend Television's *South Bank Show*, 19 November 1995.

## 4   Building community

1   M. Scott Peck, *The Different Drum* (Rider, 1987).

2   Scott Peck, *The Different Drum*.

3   James O'Halloran, *Small Christian Communities* (Columba Press, 1996).

4   Scott Peck, *The Different Drum*.

5   Beesing, Nogosek and O'Leary, *The Enneagram: A Journey of Self Discovery* (Dimension Books, 1984). Also Myers Briggs: Kiersey and Bates, *Please Understand Me* (Nemesis Books, 1978).

## 5   The whole of life

1   Pierre Gerety was killed in the Swissair plane crash off Nova Scotia in September 1998. He was little known to many outside the aid and development agency world, but he was a tireless 'champion of the poor'.

Peter read about him in the *Guardian* obituary page. Pierre Gerety is once reported to have said: 'When the law is on your side, argue the law: when the facts are on your side, argue the facts: when neither is on your side, take off your shoe and bang it on the table!' There are many such inspirational people around – and surprisingly, the obituary columns of papers often tell very moving and inspirational stories.

2    Ann Morisy, *Beyond the Good Samaritan* (Mowbray, 1997).

3    Morisy, *Beyond the Good Samaritan.*

4    Case Study, Peter Price, 1991.

5    Article by Carlos Mesters in *Christian* 1/98. He has developed this thinking in a number of places, most notably in *God, Where Are You? Rediscovering the Bible* (Orbis, 1995).

## 6    Making a difference

1    Sharon D. Welch, *A Feminist Ethic of Risk* (Augsburg-Fortress, 2000).

2    Kathy Galloway (ed.), *Starting Where We Are* (Wild Goose Publications, 1998).

3    Adapted from Terry Veiling, *Living in the Margins – Intentional Communities and the Art of Interpretation* (Crossroad/Herder, 1996).

4    Arthur Baranowski, *Creating Small Faith Communities* (St Anthony Messenger Press).

5    The New Way publications listed in the Resources section offer tools for reflection on all four gospels.

6    Schreiter, *Constructing*, pp. 17–18.

7    Schreiter, *Constructing*, p. 20.

## 7    A new way of being local church

1    Walter Wink, *Engaging the Powers.*

2    *Sojourners*, October 1990.

3    From Peter's commonplace book.

4    'Targeting priorities', Carol Stickland in *A Tapestry of Stories* (New Way Publications, 1999).

5    Jeanne Hinton, *Changing Churches: Building Bridges in Local Mission* (CTBI, 2002).

6    *Church at the Most Local Level: A pastoral priority shaping the Catholic Church in East Africa.* Report by Jeanne Hinton on visit in Spring 2002.

7    Magdalen Smith, *Celebration: Fiesta Fun for Small Christian Communities* (New Way Publications, 2000).

8    Leonardo Boff, *Ecclesio-Genesis: The base communities reinvent the church* (Collins, 1996).

# Resources

## Books

Simon Barrow, *Expanding Horizons: Learning to be the Church in the World*, Church in Society Publications, 1995.

Simon Barrow (ed.), *Summarizing 'Building Bridges of Hope'*, CTBI, 2001.

Steve Croft, *Transforming Communities: Re-imaging the Church in the 21st Century*, DLT, 2002.

Ciarnan Earley and Gemma McKenna, *Actions Speak Louder*, Columba Press, 1987. *Useful resource book on the pastoral cycle and social analysis.*

Ian Fraser, *Reinventing Church: Insights from Small Christian Communities and Reflections on a Journey Among Them*, Iona Community, 2002.

Kathy Galloway, *Starting Where We Are, The Story of a Neighbourhood Centre*, Wild Goose Publications, 1989.

Laurie Green, *Let's Do Theology*, Mowbray, 1999.

Margaret Hebblethwaite, *Basic is Beautiful*, Fount/Chapman, 1986.

– *Base Communities*, Fount/Chapman, 1986.

Jeanne Hinton, *Walking in the Same Direction: A New Way of Being Church*, WCC Risk Publications, 1995.

– *Changing Churches: Building Bridges in Local Mission*, CTBI, 2002. *Also see New Way Publications below.*

Joe Holland and Peter Henriot, *Social Analysis/Linking Faith and Justice*, Orbis, 1980.

Anthony J. Gittins, *Bread for the Journey – the Transformation of Mission and the Mission of Transformation*, Orbis, 1996.

Jose Marins, Teolide Maria Trevisan and Carloee Chanona, *The Church from the Roots: Basic Ecclesial Communities*, CAFOD, 1989.

David Martin and Simon Barrow, *Bridges to Build: Group Learning Sessions*, CTBI, 2001.

Maylanne Maybee (ed.), *All Who Minister: New Ways of Serving God's People*, Anglican Book Centre, Canada, 2001.

Carlos Mesters, *Defenseless Flower: New Reading of the Bible*, Orbis, 1989.
– *God, Where Are You? Rediscovering the Bible*, Orbis, 1995.

Mission Theological Advisory Group, *Presence and Prophecy: A Heart for Mission in Theological Education*, Church House Publishing/CTBI, 2002.

– *The Search for Faith and the Witness of the Church*, Church House Publishing, 1996.

Ann Morisy, *Beyond the Good Samaritan: Community, Ministry and Mission*, Mowbray, 1997.

Ched Myers et. al., edited Karen Lattea, *Say to this Mountain: Mark's Story of Discipleship*, Orbis, 1996.

– *Binding the Strong Man: A Political Reading of Mark's Gospel*, Orbis, 1989. *These two books of biblical studies are worth their weight in gold!*

Jim O'Halloran, *Signs of Hope: Developing Small Christian Communities*, Orbis, 1991.

– *Small Christian Communities: A Pastoral Companion*, Orbis, 1996.

Peter B. Price, *Seeds of the Word: Biblical Reflections for Small Church Communities*, DLT, 1996.

– *Undersong: Listening to the Soul*, DLT, 2002.

– *Praying the Blue Note*, DLT, 2002.

*See also New Way publications below.*

Robert Schreiter, *Constructing Local Theologies*, SCM Press, 1985.

Jim Wallis, *Faith Works*, SPCK, 2002.

Evelyn Eaton Whitehead and James Whitehead, *Community of Faith: Models and Strategies for Developing Christian Communities*, Winston & Seabury, 1982.

Walter Wink, *Engaging the Powers*, Fortress, 1992. *And other books by the same author developing the theme of God's 'domination free order'.*

## Other resources

**A New Way of Being Church** is a network of people who seek to co-operate with Jesus Christ in the formation of God's new order of justice, love and peace. We encourage people engaged in transforming the places where they live and work into communities of hope by providing workshops, publications and a resource library. Further information can be obtained from our website: www.newway.org.uk, or by writing to New Way, The Palace, Wells, Somerset BA5 2PD.

**New Way Publications** include a series of biblical reflections for small Christian communities by Peter Price. These booklets cover all four gospels. The most recent New Way publication is *Stepping Stones: Stories Along the Way*, edited by Jeanne Hinton. Write to New Way for a complete list of publications, or see our website: www.newway.org.uk.

**New Way Resources** is a collection of articles, books, case studies, reports and stories from around the world, illustrating a new way of being church. Visitors are welcome to arrange a time to come to the New Way office and work with these materials.

# Some other useful networks are:

**Building Bridges of Hope,**
www.geocities.com/ccom_ctbi/Building_Bridges_of_Hope.html
Building Bridges of Hope is a process for accompanying and
supporting a range of over twenty creative experiments in emergent
or existing forms of church life across England, Scotland, Wales and
Ireland. It aims to discover how ground-up initiatives can help change
the wider culture of institutional church life. Building Bridges of Hope
is sponsored by the ecumenical Churches' Commission on Mission in
association with ecumenical and denominational bodies and agencies
throughout Britain and Ireland. It is based on indicators derived from
detailed research among diverse congregations between 1996–2000. A
video, workbook and book (Jeanne Hinton's *Changing Churches* – see
bibliography) are available. See the website for more details or contact
the Revd Terry Tennens (terry.tennens@tesco.net).

**Grassroots**, 47 High Town Rd, Luton LU2 0BW.

**The Iona Community**, The Abbey, Iona, Argyll PA76 6SN.

**National Justice and Peace Network**, 39 Eccleston Square, London
SW1V 1BX.

**Living Spirituality Network**, The Well at Willen, Milton Keynes
MK15 9AA.

**National Association of Christian Communities and Networks**
(NACCAN), Community House, Eton Road, Newport NP9 OBL.